DEVON MYSTERIES

Judy Chard

D1494766

BOSSINEY BOOKS

First published in 1979
by Bossiney Books
St Teath, Bodmin, Cornwall
Typeset and printed in Great Britain by
Penwell Ltd., Parkwood, Callington,
Cornwall

ISBN 0 906456 29 0

PLATE ACKNOWLEDGMENTS

Cover photograph by David Golby
1, 22 Arthur Bebbings
10, 11, 13, 15 The Author
12, 16, 17, 18, 19, 20 David Golby
4, 5 by courtesy of Warren House Inn
7 by courtesy of Tavistock Inn
21 by courtesy of Robert Hatch
8, 9, 14 Mary Pierce
3 Paul Broadhurst
2 Chris Chapman
6 Ray Bishop

ABOUT THE AUTHOR

Devon is not only a beautiful county, it's a mysterious place too — and if anybody had any doubts about that, Judy Chard demolishes them with her exploration into the strange and often the inexplicable. This book though is not just about *mysterious Devon*, it's essentially about *Devon mysteries.*

Some of her stories begin as legends but as they take shape and substance one wonders if there can be any smoke without fire, any genuine myth without a degree of reality. In others, Judy Chard charts factual events that defy human explanation, and as a novelist she knows better than most that the line dividing fact and fiction is frequently blurred.

Here a writer, with rare insight and objectivity, introduces us to the truly mysterious face of Devon. A book to make the cynics think again — and a good read for all who love the eerie side of Westcountry Life.

Judy Chard contributes each month to *Devon Life.* A prolific writer: novelist, short story author, journalist and broadcaster, this is her fourth title for Bossiney Books. She made her Bossiney debut in the autumn of 1978 with *Along the Lemon,* following it with *Along the Dart,* both of which were well received and both of which were the subject of a five-episode series on BBC's *Morning SouWest.* More recently, Bossiney published her *About Widecombe,* which has been called 'a beautiful portrait of a beautiful Devonshire village'. In it she interviews well-known characters and tells the story of the world-famous Widecombe Fair.

DEVON MYSTERIES

Out of the mists of Devon and Dartmoor, in particular, from the rugged tors and the deep coombes come stories and legends. Some in this book have been told or added to by friends — old and new, some of whom wish to remain anonymous — and most have been experienced by the story tellers themselves.

In other cases, I have researched and have tried to follow up by visiting the area or house concerned to update information where-ever possible. I had to be on the alert for fabrication, but one thing did stand out during the interviews: all the people I talked to had an utter sincerity and a belief in what they told me, and more often than not their story was confirmed either by someone else or factual evidence from my own research. Perhaps some of the experiences seem a little slight, but because of that very fact they speak to me of truth, for why make up something trivial?

Because of modern education and scientific fact the supernatural is less talked about today, but isn't it rather significant that UFOs and the Bermuda Triangle have appeared in their place? That is why a chapter on the former is included in this book, for there have been hundreds of local sightings.

Murder and suicide, of course, often lead to rumours of hauntings. Perhaps the very fact that they are horrifying makes us feel some-thing supernatural must have been left, as in the most terrifying example at Castel-a-Mare in Torquay, which I investigated with rather odd results!

In common with many people, I think it possible violence may leave an imprint on the surroundings by the emotions released at the time of the actual happening. What are radio and TV but a kind of imprint on the ether which travels on a particular wavelength? I see no reason to deny psychic phenomena nor cosmic consciousness when man's mind may merge with a kind of Universal Intelligence, even if only for a flash of a second. Many deep thinking people feel there are earthbound spirits which can be benign or a real danger to anyone, for instance, using a Ouija Board, the same spirits perhaps who are said to manifest in a house and cause disturbances and fear, maybe with no intention of harming people physically but attempting perhaps to draw attention to the frustration they experience in not being able to communicate with or be seen by the particular occupier of the house.

I don't think hauntings just occur — I think some particular physical presence is needed to cause an apparition to appear. Maybe there are people who attract the past in some way so that exorcism, if it is practised, has its effect on the people at the place and not on the supposed spirits. As a water diviner I know everything has its 'field' or aura, so perhaps evil or good can impress itself and cause this atmosphere that many people feel. Some buildings seem to oppress us with a sense of the people who have lived and died in them. It isn't so very hard to understand, for the walls and floors and ceilings of old buildings must be saturated with the exhalations of human emotions. I read somewhere the theory that a shadow that once falls on a wall leaves a shadow there forever.

To be honest I have seen neither ghost nor UFO, neither do I know how water divining occurs although I can dowse in a very amateur way, neither do I understand how a coloured picture is brought to my room from thousands of miles away by satellite — so I shall repeat the well worn quotation that 'there are more things in heaven and earth, Horatio, than are dreamed of in your philosophy'. In that period of my life when I worked in a city, if someone had told me there were people who could cure warts by remote control, ill-wish their neighbour's pig, or see pixies on Dartmoor, I should have fallen about laughing, but not now, I have talked to too many people who have convinced me of such things, and maybe when you have read some of my experiences you too will not be so inclined to scoff as you may have been before you picked up this book. Perhaps even on some twilit evening you may look twice over your shoulder as you come down off Dartmoor, not quite sure if that granite rock really is a stone or if it moved slightly.

As witchcraft has flourished in Devon ever since history was first recorded, let us look at witches, and pixies, and cures and curses.

WITCHES' BREW

'For my part I have ever believed and do now know that there are witches.'

So said Sir Thomas Browne in the seventeenth century, but witchcraft has always flourished. King Saul consulted the Witch of Endor and Emperor Augustus of Rome had his own private soothsayers. Browne himself had a curiously mixed nature; although by training he was a scientist and philosopher, he was also a mystic and extremely credulous.

It's difficult to appreciate how powerful was the influence of witchcraft on the lives of the people of this country during the middle ages — or is it? Today in Africa there are still witch doctors in spite of a veneer of civilisation. They probably hold sway over people mainly by the skilful effects and exploitation of auto-suggestion — how about Hitler? Recently a book was published called *Witch Amongst Us* by Lois Bourne in which she states she is a witch and goes on to prove it! The Act which made witchcraft a capital offence was removed from the statute book in 1736, the last woman executed for this crime in Devon being Alice Molland, hanged at Exeter in March 1694, but the *Transactions of the Devonshire Association* give many later examples of witchcraft. To quote just one, said to have taken place in 1820, when two witches, a man called Durke and his wife, and a widowed sister-in-law, Deb Knight, were involved. This was written up in 1882. Then in 1879 a Dartmoor farmer, who had lost a lot of cattle, killed a sheep and burned it on the moor above his farm as a sacrifice — soon after his cattle recovered fully.

Probably the most famous witchcraft trial in Devon took place in 1682 when three Bideford witches, Temperance Lloyd, Susanna Edwards and Mary Trembles, were condemned to death and executed at Exeter.

One of the Frenches of Oakford kept losing his cattle and he called on a white witch for advice. Algy May, who lives at Rowbrook Farm, told me that Canon Hall, now retired and living at Leusdon, remembers seeing a dried up piece of liver in a recess by the farm hearth, for it was believed evil spells could be broken by pins stuck into the heart of a freshly killed sheep or bullock, and often too a liver was used.

Percy Braund of Broadhempston told me: 'My granny could work cures. When I was fourteen I went to live at Cordonford Farm near Cator Court for eighteen months. I cleaned out the shippon mornings — the cattle lived-in in winter — and I used to go down to Ponsworthy for the newspaper and groceries from the shop. One of the papers I picked up was the *Daily Express* sent every Wednesday from London by someone who never forgot what she owed my gran, Mrs Turner. This woman's daughter's face was in a terrible state with erysipelas and gran cured it. This girl came over to the farm three or four days — I saw her as I cleaned out the shippon — gran took her into a little room where no one else was allowed. She used blackthorn and milk and said a prayer . . . it's so vivid in my mind . . . by the fourth day she hadn't a mark on her skin, that girl.' Elizabeth Turner did many cures, skin diseases being her chief thing, and Percy said, 'I know this was only an incident, but I've carried it all my life, that she could be cured in such a short time.'

Once every village had at least two witches. They studied the weather, practised healing with herbs and were held in great awe by their innocent neighbours, which innocence of course they played on. This belief lasted longer in the Westcountry than anywhere else, possibly because John Wesley believed in the evil side of witchcraft, saying that to deny its existence was to deny the teachings of Exodus. However nowadays white witches in Devon are ordinary people who happen to have some kind of mysterious power and also use their natural gifts to make use of it for healing and blessing. The gift is passed from man to woman until one member of the family is found who can use it.

Witches have always used saliva very freely both for charms and curses thinking it holds the essence of personality and it is a quite horrifying fact that very recently a young policeman died as a result of being spat upon at a football match by a hooligan. The verdict was that he had contracted meningitis from the spittal.

There are of course black, white and grey witches, the names being self explanatory, and the evil eye or ill-wishing is interestingly explained — or at least one theory of it given — in an account of a lecture by an American professor describing that yeast cells can be killed by the glance of a person looking at them intently for a few minutes. Perhaps certain rays emitted from human eyes, as well as from other parts of the body, can cause actual physical change. How about a sheepdog who can hold sheep with his eyes? And the case of the woman who took my grandmother to court because she said her red setter dog had 'held her with its eyes' in the lane outside our house and so terrified her she had a miscarriage.

Surely this idea and feel for witchcraft would not have still survived if there wasn't at least something in it, and after all how often one sees the natural force come first to be eventually confirmed by scientific fact. Once we thought carrots being good for the eyesight was an old wives' tale, but it has been proved in the lab. that they hold vitamins which benefit the eye. Recently Patricia Jackson writing in the *Daily Mail* says of old wives' remedies: 'while many of them may be dismissed as superstitious nonsense, scientific research is proving some to have a basis of truth. A doctor claimed recently that the old wives' cure of hot chicken soup to relieve mucous congestion really worked . . .' Seaweed and moss have always been thought beneficial to those with chest complaints and she says: 'If you look on the shelves of most health food shops today seaweed derivatives are similarly recommended.' And I myself have a very down-to-earth friend whose wife tried every doctor's remedy for her bronchitis without success, but two cloves of raw garlic eaten at bed time have completely cured it.

In the past it seems most black witches were women, and more men the white variety, and even the medical profession came under their spell to a certain extent as is shown by the following.

In 1917 a Dr Gidley of Cullompton wrote up a case (vol. 49 pp 69-71 *Transactions of the Devonshire Association*) describing how he came in contact with white witchcraft in 1897. 'Twenty years ago,' he wrote, 'I was consulted by a woman suffering from a growth (suspiciously cancerous) in the breast. I advised her to lose no time in undergoing an operation and as a result she went to the Tiverton Hospital, but in the meantime she met someone who told her she could cure her before she went in for the operation as she "knew something — a certain person was evil wishing her". The woman determined to give a trial to the performance advocated by her friend. She procured a sheep's heart and at a certain hour of the night, stuck pins in it reciting some such formula as "May each pin: thus stuck in this poor heart: in hers to go who hurts me so till she departs." The heart and its pins were to be placed upon the bar that holds up the pot hooks in the chimney and left there . . . the curious part of this story is that a certain woman in the neighbourhood became ill and weak, and eventually died; still more curious is that synchronously with that person's increasing feebleness the growth in the breast of the other woman dwindled and disappeared. It was not for some 3 or 4 years that I saw her again after she left me to make the appointment at the hospital, and I was anxious to know by what means the trouble had been overcome . . . reticent at first, eventually she told me the facts and lived ten years after.'

Dr Gidley himself died at Heyford House, Cullompton on 15 January 1938.

Of course the distinction between the black and white witches is obviously that the former use their power for evil and are extremely malignant, whilst the white work magic for the benefit of their neighbours and can disperse the evil of the other, whilst the grey ones possess a double power and perhaps most of all can either 'overlook' or 'release'.

As recently as 1924 a method was still in use to find out if a person was a witch. If someone thought they were bewitched, they attacked the suspect with a new nail or pin and drew blood above the nose, and then if the spell was broken this proved it was witchcraft! From the *Devonshire Transactions* (vol. 57 p. 18) comes an account of a man charged at Cullompton Petty Sessions on Monday 8 December 1924 with assaulting a woman on 21 November. He said the woman had ill-wished him and bewitched his pig. Alfred John Matthews aged 43, smallholder, living at Clyst St Lawrence was summoned by Ellen Garnsworthy, a middle-aged married woman living two doors away, alleging common assault, saying he had scratched her with a pin as she passed his door on the way to fetch water. He had said, 'Perhaps that'll teach you to leave other people's things alone!' She said she'd never touched anything of his and didn't understand what he meant. He had then said, 'I have something else inside for you!' She had thought he meant a gun and told her husband. The defendant admitted scratching her with a pin, one stroke on each hand.

One of the magistrates asked if he alleged she was a witch.

'Yes!' said Matthews.

'Such a fallacy died out years ago,' he was told.

'Not with some of us it hasn't!' was the retort.

He got a month's imprisonment. Old beliefs die hard. We all know only too well that black magic is still practised in many places — the veneer of civilisation is thinner than we think.

Sabine Baring Gould must be one of the sources of tales of witches par excellence and in his *Devonshire Characters* he tells of an old woman who was a white witch and received presents from all the farmers in the district to keep her sweet! Should she meet a child coming from school and 'fix her with her eye' she would probably say, 'My dear, I knawes a chiel like you, same age, red rosy cheeks and curling black hair, and 'er shrivelled up, shrumped like an apple as is picked in the third quarter of the moon. Cheeks grew white, hair went out of curl, and she just died . . .'

Before the day was out a chicken or a batch of eggs arrived as a present from the child's mother. The witch lived in a ruined cottage with no roof, saying 'God made the sky, the best roof of all,' refusing all offers of repairs from the farmers, and even the vicar himself. To their entreaties she replied, ''There be angels every night sits on the rungs of the ladder to my bedroom to see nobody comes nigh me, and ready to hold up the timbers so they don't fall on me.' Eventually she had to live downstairs in a kind of lean-to hut for several winters including the terrible one of 1893/4, taking refuge in an old oak chest, keeping the lid up with a brick. Then the place caught fire and she was taken to the workhouse.

Of course it was no uncommon sight in those days for the local postman to be seen walking with one hand extended, holding a handkerchief to be blessed by the white witch, it being essential no other human hand touched it before it reached her!

WART CHARMING AND PIXIES

I too have my own story of a white witch or wart charmer. In the days when I still had dogs, one of them developed thirteen of these pests. My vet. said, 'Nothing much I can do, try a wart charmer,' and gave me an address to visit on the moor. He warned me, of course, I must not offer any money — that would be an insult. After an appropriate distance of time a bottle of whisky or some tobacco at Christmas could be given tactfully, but if a witch takes money his powers will leave him. Not only is this power highly prized and safeguarded, but it is at the disposal free for anyone who asks. In this case it was a lady I was to visit. The thatched cottage stood by itself a little way beyond the village, a rowan and elder tree growing either side of the gate. Mountain ash is a powerful plant used in witchcraft and was often carried in processions as a protection against evil in the early days of Christianity. A mass of marigolds grew everywhere — standing for happiness in herb law. I had read recently they are the only flowers considered safe to be left in a sick room as they have been proved to have healing powers. Herbs too grew in profusion including borage, the bees' favourite plant often given to those who have had a death in the family — a joyful herb inspiring courage.

The door opened. Surely this was a witch in true tradition. Thin wisps of grey hair framed a gaunt face and one glass eye of fixed intent did nothing to dispel the impression.

'Come in little maid,' she said, as though I was expected. The light was dim, a log fire crackled in the grate, by the window stood a table covered with a scarlet chenille cloth and glass cabinets held silver cups and china, photos and a huge ostrich egg. For a while we talked trivia, parrying round the subject of warts, until at last I told her why I had come and she said, as it happened, she could cure warts, but this was the least among her gifts. She could cure many bodily illnesses and treat those suffering from bad luck, bad temper, jealousy and unrequited love. She could turn the dislike of relatives so that wills might be altered, and break spells cast by her black sisters and brothers, her white or natural magic being wrought entirely for good. She had 'reached out' to Australia and cured a young man of 34 who was 'mazed' in the head and returned him, sane and healthy, to his mother in the village — I could ask anyone I liked for confirmation.

I wouldn't dare . . .

She got up and took me to the window, pointing to a holly hedge — seven trees with an elderberry and white thorn at the end. Under this latter a portion had been cut away from the lower branches so a person could stand upright in its shade, here to be cured of skin diseases.

She went out of the room and came back with a rusty tin. For a moment I had visions of bat's wings, toad's legs and hare's blood, but it proved to be nothing worse than a dock root.

'Go home and dig up a big dock like this, don't let 'ee bleed mind, then wash off the earth, chop'n into a saucepan and bring to the boil. Keep it going for ten minutes, and when it's cool put three drops on each wart. Now mind, they warts may be seven, eleven or seventeen days going, no telling. Just have to wait. Tell me how many there are.'

'Thirteen.' I knew numbers in wart charming are very important.

'At ten o'clock tonight think of me and repeat aloud the Lord's Prayer.' She wrote my name in a little black book crammed with thick writing like a plum cake with fruit, adding Fred, my dog's name and the number of warts.

I dug up an enormous dock and carried out her instructions to the letter. I resisted all temptation to examine the warts for a week. Then one day I was brushing the other dog, Ollie, and found a large seedy wart on his head. Quickly I searched Fred. Every wart had gone — Ollie had thirteen!

Of course there are hundreds of cures for warts and it seems only the charmer needs to have complete faith as so often it is animals who are in need of the cure. Could it be simply thought transference or some form of telepathy and was this what had happened to my dogs? I don't know, I simply didn't have the nerve to go back. Skin diseases of all sorts are cured by these people such as erysipelas, as in the case of Percy Braund's gran, and shingles. All these are surface ailments, so perhaps the natural, untrained healer can only get results in these cases. The late Vian Smith, whom I admired greatly, tells in his book *Portrait of Dartmoor* of Mr Brackenbury from the Ring O' Bells pub at North Bovey whose wife bought a mare called Double Brown at the Exeter horse sales in 1956. She only gave 35 guineas for it as it was bone thin and had warts on its stomach and foreleg.

Mrs Brackenbury tried several cures without success, and then she visited a wart charmer at Westcott. However he was away from home, but when he was told of her visit later he said it did not matter as he could cure by remote control. Within ten days every wart had gone. It could be coincidence . . . on the other hand . . .

One old and tried cure is to take from a running stream some small stones equal in number to the warts, put them in a clean white bag and throw them in the road. The warts will then be transferred to whoever picks them up. Rather unkind I feel, but it has taught me never to pick up a white bag I may see in the road.

A wreath or ring of rushes placed over the affected area and then hung up inside the chimney is said to be very effective. In *Nummits and Crummits* by Sarah Hewett she gives pages of cures and charms, and one that particularly intrigued me was to take an eel and cut off the head, rub the warts with the blood, and bury the head in the ground. When it has rotted the warts will fall off. There are many variations on this theme, beef or a toad being used. I prefer the idea that a rose picked on Midsummer Day and packed away undisturbed will be as fresh as ever on Christmas Day and if worn to church the girl's lover will come and take it from her.

Many country people still use the Bible as a method of telling the future, opening it at random and trying to find some clue in the first words to meet the eye.

To cure 'Zweemy headedness — and we can all guess what caused that — wash the head with plenty of old rum, the back and face with sour wine, wear flannel next to the skin and carry a packet of salt in the left hand pocket. I think maybe I'll take an aspirin instead.

To keep fleas away — when you hear the first cuckoo take some of the earth from the place on which your right foot is standing and sprinkle on the threshold of your front door, but tell no one. No fleas, beetles, earwigs or vermin will cross it. I don't know quite what you do if it is winter when these pests appear and the cuckoo still in Africa!

To cure that nagging tooth, cut toe and finger nails, take the parings, wrap in tissue and put into a slit made in the bark of an ash tree before sunrise. You will never have toothache as long as you live!

I like this clue to the superstition that it is unlucky to open an umbrella indoors. There is an entry in the parish accounts of St Andrews Church, Plymouth, for 1749 mentioning the expenditure of 16/- on a parish umbrella for the use of the minister at burials. Originally the only umbrellas that were known in England were those used by the parson on rainy days at funerals, so one can now understand why it became an omen of death for one to be opened inside the house.

Of course, in Devon we know the county was once cursed by the Druids and mistletoe was forbidden to grow in it. It is odd that a man who had an orchard, one half of which was in Devon and the other just over the border in Somerset — the division marked by a ditch — could grow mistletoe on the trees in the Somerset half but not on those on the Devon side. I still know people who make a habit of sowing garden seeds on Good Friday, who are thrilled to meet a flock of sheep on the road when on a journey and to hear crickets in the house. In a more macabre mood, it is said to be lucky to possess a rope by which a person has been hanged — more of this later — but it is unlucky to look back when leaving the house, or to eat fish from the head down. To cure a sore throat you simply repeat the eighth psalm seven times for three successive mornings over the patient. If your nose bleeds take one or two fine old toads — the next part is not for the squeamish — and place them in a cold oven. Increase the heat until sufficiently fierce to cook the toads and reduce them to a brown, crisp mass. Remove them from the oven and beat them to a powder in a stone mortar. Place the powder in a box and use as snuff.

Have you ever heard of anything more revolting and cruel? It's enough to give you diarrhoea at the thought, and if it does, then take a stale Good Friday cross bun and place it too in a hot oven to dry. Grate when hard into powder, make into a paste with water and take to cure this complaint. For whooping cough, bring an ass before the door of the house into whose mouth thrust a new slice of bread, then pass the sick child three times over and under the animal's body, and the charm is complete. When I was a child we were walked briskly round the gas works. I don't know of either

14

cure actually working.

To see if you will marry, on Christmas Eve go into the yard and rap smartly on the door of the hen house. If a hen cackles first you will never marry, but if a cock crows, then you will marry before the end of the coming year.

Perhaps the most important cure of all is to destroy the power of a witch. In three small-necked stone jars place liver of frog stuck with new pins, heart of toad stuck with thorns from a holy thorn bush, cork and seal. Bury in three different churchyard paths seven inches from the surface and seven feet from the porch. Repeat the Lord's Prayer backwards as you do so. As the hearts and livers decay, so will the witch's power vanish.

Strangely enough, in spite of its wildness and loneliness, Dartmoor doesn't have a wide range of legends and hauntings, although Devon is rich in folklore, superstition and mystery. It isn't difficult to imagine one hears the wish huntsmen and hounds when the wind shrieks and snowflakes whirl. You'd think the tors and valleys, shaded glens and wooded ravines would be alive with ghosts and hauntings, but really there are only a few which are repeated and told over and over again, and most of these are connected either with the Devil or Pixies. Every moorman worth his salt believes in the little people of Devon, ugly little men, sometimes dressed in rags, sometimes in green and scarlet, sometimes timid and shy. They can be friendly but must not be trifled with as you may then become pixie-led as did a Mrs G. Herbert. Mr Coxhead describes her experience in 1928 in the *Transactions of the Devonshire Association*. She met a pixie on Dartmoor near Shaugh Bridge in 1897, a wizened little man eighteen inches high. She became 'mazed and befogged' and realising she was being pixie-led, turned her pockets inside out to break the spell. Immediately all her senses returned, so beware of their favourite haunts which are New Bridge, Huccaby Cleave, Sheeps Tor and Pixie's Holt.

Some say these little people are the souls of unchristened babies, more like mischievous children than harmful. One of the most famous and oft-told legends regarding them concerns Tom White of Postbridge. One night he had been to visit his sweetheart, a dairy-maid at Huccaby farm five miles away. It was a summer evening and he had stayed late so that it was past midnight when he kissed his love good night and set out for home.

The night was mild and starry. He was walking across the moor

15

with Bellever Tor looming against the starlight, Laughter Tor gradually melting into the ridge of Hameldown, not enough wind to shake a cobweb, when suddenly he stopped dead in his tracks at the sound of laughter, shrill and clear. And then he saw them — hundreds of little creatures no higher than his knee, dressed in green and dancing in a ring on a smooth piece of turf. They drew him into the dance before he could resist, leaping and laughing, whirling and shouting. He told them he had no intention of spying, but they took no notice, making him dance till dawn when he sank to the ground more dead than alive. He swore he'd go no more accourting — and he didn't. He died a bachelor. History doesn't relate what happened to his sweetheart.

When the Fernworthy Reservoir was made to provide water for Torquay, opened in 1942, the ancient farmhouse had to be demolished. It had last been occupied in 1928, and its former site on the north west bank of the reservoir is commemorated by a pixie legend. The house was built in 1590 by the last male member of a yeoman family, on the site of a much older house which had been in his family for generations. Built of Dartmoor granite, stark and gloomy, it was much resented by the pixies who did not like human beings on their territory. The rocks in the area were under their protection, and they vowed vengeance on the builder.

Soon after the man and his wife moved in, a son was born, and one winter evening the wife sat by the peat fire, rocking the cradle while her man was out tending his cattle. The door was ajar, the warmth of the fire made her drowsy and she fell asleep. She woke with a start just in time to see a grey cloak disappear and hear a weird laugh of triumph. Her child had been stolen, never to be seen again.

A cause of some disbelief and suspicion is the ability to divine water, the art having been practised in Devon perhaps more than anywhere. During the fifteenth century dowsers were brought from Germany to Devon and Cornwall to find the lost tin mines and from them the local folk, many of whom already could divine water, also learned to find minerals. However, scientists regard belief in water divining on the same level as belief in fairies, but great reserves of water exist in rock fissures in the crust of the earth, even in the Sahara, and diviners have been able to locate these when geologists have not. Another curious mystery connected with water is the pond at North Tawton where at one time lived a family by the name of Bath and this pond was on their land. It behaved in the most curious way, for when the weather was dry it was full of water, and often empty when it rained. It was said to be very deep in the middle, deep enough to cover a man mounted on a horse. It filled itself apparently when a calamity was about to occur, either in the family or in the life of the nation, and it has been said that it did indeed foretell in this manner the deaths of George IV, Edward VII, George V and the Queens Charlotte and Victoria, also the Duke of Wellington.

There are, too, many tales in connection with magic circles of stones and rocks, and the Aetherius Society visits Dartmoor in an effort to raise energy and power towards the prohibition of atom bomb tests. They consider certain hills to be natural reservoirs of this energy, and they stand in a circle with upraised hands, their bodies acting as power conductors. This in a way leads me to talk of other powers, darker than these, of the Devil, with whom the people of Devon seem to have something of an obsession.

THE DEVIL IN DEVON

A moorland farmer riding home from Widecombe full of cider, saw the wish hounds in Wistman's wood and said, 'Hey there old Nick, have a good run? Did you kill?' And the ghostly huntsman said 'Yes, and here's one of them,' and he threw the farmer the corpse of a small child which, to his horror, the farmer saw was his own son. There are many stories like this — but it seems the Devil made two major visits to Devon apart from the minor ones.

The first was the most terrifying and took place on 21 October 1638 during the worst storm ever recorded in the United Kingdom. There are of course dozens of different accounts of this, but the most usual concerns a local ne'er-do-well, Widecombe Jan, who had made a pact with the Devil to the effect that if ever he was found by that lord of the underworld asleep in the church he could have his soul — to me this seems a rather cheap price! However, he was indeed found asleep, maybe after too good a Devon Sunday lunch, the usual pack of playing cards in his hand. A short while before this, at the Tavistock Inn at Poundsgate, a man dressed all in black and riding a jet black horse had stopped to ask the way to Widecombe. He ordered a pint of ale and to the landlord's consternation, as the liquid went down the stranger's throat, it hissed as though quenching flames and not a thirst! Finishing the drink, the man threw some coins on the counter, mounted his horse and was gone, but no sooner had the clatter of hooves died away than the landlord saw the money had turned to dried leaves in his hand!

Meanwhile down in Widecombe church the Reverend George Lyde was conducting the afternoon service, probably many of the congregation drowsing as was Jan. Suddenly the sky went black; in fact inside the church it was so dark people could hardly see each other. The service faltered for lack of light. Then the church was lit by blue flames, a ball of fire burst through one of the windows and passed down the nave, and those who could, fell on their knees, certain the Day of Judgement had come.

Explosions like cannons rolled around the pillars, lightning flashed, beams crashed down, stones were shaken from the tower, one of the pinnacles collapsed. A man had his head cloven into three pieces, his hair stuck to one of the pillars with blood. Jan was killed by being dashed against another pillar. The parsons' wife was scorched, but her child next to her escaped any injury.clothes were set on fire amidst the stench of scorching flesh and fabric. Four people were killed and 62 injured. All were half crazed with terror and shock, and the church rang with the screams of people calling for God's mercy. Many died days after from burns. Some of the seats were turned completely over and yet those on them received no injury. A dog was picked up by the whirlwind which followed, thrown through the door and killed. It is really difficult to imagine the terrible scene. Then. as suddenly as it happened, the storm ceased and complete silence filled the little village. Someone at last whispered it might be as well to get out of the building, but the minister, who had stayed in his pulpit unharmed, said, 'It were better to die here than in another place.' Possibly even he was convinced the end of the world had come.

Many of the villagers were certain the experience had not just been a horrifying thunderstorm and said that Widecombe Jan — Jan Reynolds — was not killed but borne away on the back of the Devil's black horse, and that as he went he dropped the pack of cards he always carried. As they passed over Vitifer and Birch Tor, the four aces scattered on the hillside, and today you can still see the four small intakes or field enclosures, each shaped like one of the aces, as you look across from Warren Inn . . .

The Devil's next visit was of a calmer and cooler nature, but just as mysterious. On the night of Thursday 8 February 1855, there was a slight fall of snow over the county. When the locals awoke to the shining whiteness and looked from their windows they were filled with dread, verging on terror, for there were large unidentifiable marks in the snow like huge hoof prints, eight to twelve inches apart, about four by two and a half inches in size, some said like those of a donkey with one hoof. They moved in a straight line over a hundred miles both sides of the Exe estuary. Over haystacks, across streets and courts, up walls and fences, over roofs, through locked gates, without displacing anything, through town, village and hamlet.

Dozens of suggestions were put forward: a badger, a bird carrying a donkey's shoe, a kangaroo loose from a menagerie, a water bird. Farmers, engineers, naturalists, scientists all had a go, but no one came up with any feasible solution.

Eventually a posse armed with guns set off to track it through an area bounded by Exmouth, Lympstone, Woodbury, Dawlish, Torquay and Totnes. At the church in Littleham near Exmouth the marks went all around and up to the door itself. Then a rumour started in the more remote parts of the countryside, superstition became rife. Those with elder trees or ash or rowan by their gates were lucky for they kept off evil and this must be the Devil himself. The *Illustrated London News* gave the story great cover, and the *Western Times* reported a similar occurrence five years earlier in 1850 in the same place. Did the Devil really come to Devon then? Some people quoted Dr Johnson who had said once when speaking of the Widecombe tragedy, 'At supper witchcraft was introduced. Mr Crosbie said he thought it the greatest blasphemy to suppose evil spirits, counteracting the Deity, and raising storms for instance to destroy his creatures.' Johnson had replied, 'Why sir, if moral evil be consistent with the government of the Deity why may not physical evil be also consistent with it. It is not more strange that there should be evil spirits. And as to storms, we know there are such things, and it is no worse that evil spirits raise them than that they rise . . .'

There had been the legend of the Dewerstone, too. In deep snow traces of a cloven hoof and a naked human foot were found ascending to the highest summit and on stormy winter nights the wish hounds sweep through the rocky valley with cry of dogs and winding of horns.

The Devil was up to many other minor tricks. He tried to trap the soul of Bishop Bronescombe of Exeter who, in the thirteenth century, was travelling from Widecombe to Sourton and was tired and hungry, a fact he mentioned to his chaplain, adding that when Jesus was in the wilderness he had been offered bread made of stones by the Devil. He doubted very much if he'd have had the same strength of character to refuse!

Evidently it doesn't do to tempt the Lord of Misrule, even if you are the Bishop, and as he spoke a moorman appeared and offered him bread and cheese with the proviso that the Bishop must get off his horse, bow, and call him Master. It seemed a fairly mild request and his Lordship was about to do so when the chaplain saw the moorman had a cloven hoof and he cried out in horror. The Bishop made the sign of the cross and the moorman vanished. The bread and cheese turned to stones which can still be seen on the slope of the hill.

However, St Dunstan didn't do quite so well for on one occasion when he'd bought up a supply of barley for brewing beer, hoping to sell it in competition with the cider of the locals, the Devil offered to blight the apple blossom in return for his soul. The saint argued and drove a hard bargain, but eventually it was arranged the Devil should have the Saint's soul for certain days each year, and would blight the apple trees on 17, 18 and 19 May! In the nineteenth century these were known as St Dunstan's days and country folk awaited anxiously to see if the old pact held, and their apple trees would be blasted by frost! Many a time mine have been.

The Devil added to his collection of clerical souls at Dawlish where between that town and Teignmouth stand the Parson and Clerk rocks. This time the victim was a priest who had designs on becoming the Bishop of Exeter, having been promised the post when it became vacant. He was therefore delighted to hear the Bishop had been taken ill! He visited him regularly at Dawlish where he had gone to convalesce, hoping secretly to find his health had deteriorated. Crossing Haldon Hill during a thunderstorm on one of his journeys, he and his clerk lost their way, and the parson, in a fit of temper, turned on the clerk and said, 'I'd rather have the Devil himself guide me!' upon which a man appeared offering to do just that. But he guided them to the cliff where the horses plunged over and all died. The jagged rocks stand as a reminder of the grisly end of the two men whose bodies were never found, only those of their horses at the foot of the cliffs.

There are many minor superstitions connected with the Devil such as the fact that he arrives in Devon on 20 September each year and spits on blackberries making them unfit to eat, and they do usually become tasteless and infested with maggots after that date.

In Shebbear stands the stone dropped by the Devil when he was flying through the air in a temper, a thing he seems often to have done. So on 5 November the men of the village ring the church bells and then visit the stone, heaving it over on its other side. They then return to the church to ring another peal to bring good luck to the village.

James Hannaford who died in 1899 and is buried at Widecombe

was crossing Hameldown one night from Warren House Inn to his home when he fell down an old mine shaft and was caught on some woodwork. He could see nothing but heard water dripping around him. His faithful collie stayed on the brink of the shaft all night howling to keep the Devil at bay, and at length he attracted a search party to the shaft. James was rescued but the exposure made him a cripple and he and his dog can be seen limping along the ridge on dark nights ... so they say.

JUST MACABRE

Not really for the imaginative or nervous, the first story is about the man they couldn't hang. John Henry Lee, or Babbacombe Lee as he was called, was the son of a yeoman farmer at Abbotskerswell near Newton Abbot. At one time he lived with his widowed mother at number 3, Town Cottages, in the village. At fifteen he had gone to work for Miss Keyse in her thatched house by the sea in Babbacombe. She was a lady of great distinction, rich, kind and well loved in St Marychurch.

John worked for her for eighteen months. Perhaps the gentle lap of the sea against the garden walls of the house, the sight of the big ships passing on the horizon and the talk of the local fishermen all had an effect on him, for he joined the Royal Navy. Unfortunately he had a weak chest and the tough life was too much for him. He developed pneumonia and to his great disappointment was invalided out. Had this not happened, perhaps none of the rest of the horrifying story might have occurred either.

He got into trouble for stealing from his next employer and was sent to prison for six months hard labour. When Miss Keyse heard of this she wrote to the Governor saying she would give him a job as a gardener and be responsible for him.

So his twentieth year passed in comparative peace. He courted a local girl and all seemed normal, but then in the early hours of 15 November 1884 one of the maids woke suddenly to smell smoke. The household was roused and five separate fires were found to have been started with paraffin. Then someone screamed, for in a pool of blood in the diningroom lay the body of Emma Keyse, with terrible wounds in her head and her throat slashed. Newspapers had been spread round her body but these had only smouldered making the sight for those that found her more gruesome than ever. A blood-stained towel and knife belonging to John, usually kept in his pantry,

23

were found by the body. He was arrested and charged with the murder, the motive was said to be revenge on his benefactor. He was annoyed because his weekly wage of 2s 6d had been reduced by 6d for some reason.

On 4 December he was committed for trial charged with murder.

Now comes the macabre, the unexplainable mystery.

The night before he was due to be executed, for he was found guilty, he dreamed he was on the scaffold. He heard the bolt drawn, but the trap did not open. Three times this happened, the dream being recorded in the Governor's log as true. As he was led to the scaffold the next morning, the stairs, the walls and all the ghastly details were already known to him for they were exactly as he had seen in his dream.

His legs were fastened, the rope adjusted round his neck, the cap put over his head. James Berry, the public executioner pulled the lever which freed the bolts on the trap doors. The people watching instinctively held their breath waiting for the sharp jerk, the snap of the neck bones.

The boards trembled. That was all.

Lee stood calm and erect, unruffled. Was it because of his dream he knew he would not die? Once more the whole grisly business was set in motion. Again it failed. He was taken back to his cell and the whole structure exhaustively examined. They could find nothing wrong.

He was brought back a third time. Still the trap held firmly. So John Lee went into the record books as the only man in modern legal history to be 'hanged' three times and live.

The Home Secretary signed a reprieve for life imprisonment, not a popular move for his victim had been dearly loved. Many theories were put forward for the failure of the trap door, Berry himself hinted that the instrument used on this occasion had only been used to hang a woman before and the cause of the failure was that the iron catches on the doors were not right and the woodwork should have been four times as heavy with ironwork to correspond.

Eventually released from prison Lee married Jessie Bulleid and left the district. For a short time he was a barman in a London pub. A film was made of his life story, but he did not appear in person when it was shown in Newton Abbot, although relatives from Abbotskerswell were prominent in the audience.

I went to see Mr Lang who lives in Albert Terrace in Newton Abbot and he told me, 'When I was a tacker of about eight I used to do clog dancing and play the clappers. One day down by the cross tree in Abbotskerswell, as I did my dance, a man came over and gave me half a crown, a lot of money in those days, and my mother said, "That was John Lee, the man they couldn't hang." His mother was with him. An old lady then. I always remember her hands. The skin was all brown and flabby — like stewed pears! Used to think how funny they were when I was a kid.'

I asked him if he had any theory about why John Lee didn't hang.

'No, they'd tried a sack of corn exactly his weight before hand, and it worked.' He paused: 'It was like witchcraft, that's all I can say.'

This must have been soon after Lee was released from Portland Prison for Mr Lang remembers him as being in early middle age with a bald head: 'a smallish man standing rather bewildered-looking in front of his mother's cottage.'

There's a sting in the tail which adds to the mystery. In 1936 Isadore Carter, the man who had done much to bring Lee to justice, died. Of course this revived the memory of the murder and as a result a very odd story appeared in a Torquay newspaper. 'Some time during the 1890s two young boys stood beside their father at an open grave in a local churchyard. As the coffin was lowered into the ground containing the body of a young man of good family, but insane, the older man turned to his sons and said, "Today they have buried the secret of the Babbacombe murder." '

I went down Beach Road at Babbacombe to see if I could find the thatched house where the sea washed the walls, where Emma Keyse had lain murdered while curls of smoke arose around her, but found it had been demolished. All that remains are the ruins and rubble, but as I stood there, looking out over the calm April sea thinking that once John Lee's eyes rested on exactly the same view, watching the ships, planning the murder perhaps, I couldn't help feeling a cold shiver of apprehension.

Other houses in the Torquay area have their darker side. One of these is Rock House in Maidencombe where Rudyard Kipling went to live in September 1896. At first he told his friends the place seemed almost too good to be true, for there were big sunny rooms, great trees and wide lawns dipping to the sea beneath Marychurch cliffs. Then very gradually, as if the clouds had rolled up to hide the sun, he was overcome by intense depression, caused, he said, by Feng-shui, the spirit of the house, and eventually deep deep despondency filled him which he described in *Something of Myself* (1937). Eventually this terrible despair drove the Kiplings away in the following June. As a result he wrote a psychoanalytical story, *The House Surgeon*, in which he told the story of Rock House.

On a day of just such clouds with fitful sunshine and spiteful showers I went to look at this house where he had lived and once been happy. I found it a little grim, built like a miniature castle with crenellated roof, the lane so steep I wondered how a pony and trap ever negotiated it in safety, but at least it still has its view of the sea. As I stood there I wondered if it was here he had written *Big Steamers* — 'Oh where are you going to all you Big Steamers, with England's own coal, up and down the salt seas?' — and *The Coastwise Lights* — 'The Coastwise Lights of England watch the ships of England go!'

Now we come to something even more macabre and strange, which has been described as 'Something out of Hell', a ghost so evil that it has been made immortal in all tales of the supernatural. Even before I learned the full story, and found out a little more for myself, the very name Castel-a-Mare for some reason made me shiver. But to begin at the beginning — and once again a slight confusion arises as to who actually was victim and who assassin. In one account it was said the house was owned by a local doctor who had periods of insanity and murdered his wife and also the maid who witnessed the crime, while others say it was a guest who had come as a patient to stay with him who was murdered. However after all these years perhaps the actual victim and his killer aren't as important as what they left behind. For years this old house in the Warberry area of Torquay was haunted by the maid who witnessed the brutal murder. She screamed as she saw the killing, and then turned and ran, to be chased from room to room, up and down stairs, along the dark corridors, until at last the man caught her and strangled her too, the body being put into a cupboard which was later turned into a bathroom. And so the ghost of Castel-a-Mare started to haunt the house, bringing tales of screams coming from the building at night, the stables too being affected so that horses could only be persuaded to enter backwards. A woman in velvet was seen running down the stairs shrieking, no doors stayed locked, and dogs would not pass the house without whimpering and howling.

No one would stay as tenant and eventually the house fell into disrepair, lead was stolen from the roof and the tales of horror and mystery increased.

Fascinated, I went to see Edna White, a member of the Devonshire Association who lives in Torquay. She has collected mystery stories of Devon for twenty years and she showed me some notes she had made from a book written by Violet Tweedale *Ghosts I Have Seen*. She lived in the Warberries and often passed the house. She had heard the running footsteps and the gossip about the house and went to the builder who owned it, asking if she might make some investigations.

Briefly, this is the story she tells of the three-storied house, plain and uninteresting, standing on the left-hand side of Middle Warberry Road opposite Edwinstowe, the back of the premises opening on to the road. The house was demolished in 1920 but it was in 1913 Violet Tweedale and her husband made the first investigation, which produced nothing except the chilling sensation that they were being watched by something intensely evil. Then in 1917 she was asked to join a party which intended to investigate the house with the aid of a medium. It seems a soldier home on leave was interested in psychic research and invited several people to the seance, Mrs Tweedale included.

The medium chose a bedroom on the first floor which was next to the bathroom. After some little time she suddenly started to give vent to a volley of violent language in the deep-toned voice of a man, asking what right the intruders had in his house. There was an unpleasant scene for, although the medium was a comparatively elderly and frail lady, suddenly she was controlled by this man of superhuman strength who bellowed out terrible language and then violently attacked the soldier, throwing him to the ground. Two others in the party had to go to his help, but with herculean strength the medium threw them all back against the wall, forcing them to the top of the stairs, obviously with the intention of throwing them down. There was a scuffle while the onlookers were helpless. Any moment it seemed someone would be seriously injured. Then, as suddenly as the possession had occurred, it ended; the medium crashed to the floor and it was thought she must be dead.

They picked her up and carried her into the fresh air where she gradually revived. Much to everyone's surprise, the soldier asked her if she felt inclined to undergo another experiment a few days later, and she agreed.

Once again the violence occurred, but this time the soldier was prepared; he seemed to have considerable experience and tried to exorcise the entity, whatever it might be. This led to the most incredible spiritual encounter in which it seemed first the soldier then the entity would win the fight as they swayed backwards and forwards in what can only be described as mortal combat, but at last the soldier seemed to overcome the other. The medium now started to cry. It was as if suddenly she had changed into a heartbroken young woman. She babbled incoherently between her sobs, 'Poor master . . . there on the bed . . . help him, help him.' Over and over again, she clenched her hands to her throat as if she were trying to tear away others that were attempting to strangle her, as if it were the culmination of some terrible, horrifying murder that had occurred on that very spot. Suddenly there was a piercing, bloodcurdling scream, the medium turned now as if at bay, struggling with something unseen, wrestling wildly, fighting for her very life while all the time the terrible screams came from her. The others now tried to help her, to drag her away from the invisible murderer, but it was nearly impossible to seize an intangible disembodied spirit. However, at last they managed to get the woman behind two of them against the wall so they could defend her against the first terrible spirit which had controlled her. She all the time was gasping for breath as she said hoarsely, 'He'll kill me, he's killed the master. Help, help.' But at last the soldier triumphed with his power of exorcism, if indeed that is what it was, and they managed to extract from the medium, or rather the entity which now controlled her, a few facts. Her master had been insane when the murder took place and she was the maid who had then shared the victim's fate. Mrs Tweedale goes on to say that the names and dates given were later verified from the records of the residents of the villa, but by then of course no one was left alive interested in checking up on the tragic story which was supposed to have occurred at least fifty years before. If it is true, and why should anyone doubt that it's not, it has to fall into the category of the perfect murder for no record of any murder came to the knowledge of those who were alive then.

Mrs Tweedale ends her account by saying, 'I do not know if it is intended to build another house on the same site. I hope not for it is very probable even a new residence would share the fate of the old, bricks and mortar are no impediment to the disembodied and there is no reason why they should not elect to manifest within an indefinite period of time.'

This account was dated 1920 which would make the date of the murder sometime in about 1870. Edna White told me she had tried to trace the owners and tenants of the property, but up to now all she had found was a Mrs Dove in 1857, a Mr Benjamin Fulwood in 1878/9 who were tenants. It was owned by a builder and she thinks his name was E.P.Bovey and that he lived in the house opposite, Edwinstowe. She added, 'It is probable the male victim was given a normal death certificate by the doctor who some said was a foreigner, and buried in a grave yard, although it was murder — but what happened to the body of the maid? What indeed.

Another writer was fascinated by this house, with equally disturbing results, for in his book, *Twenty-Five,* Beverly Nicholls tells how he and his brother and Lord St Audries went to explore the house one Sunday evening shortly before it was pulled down. Plaster lay about in great lumps on the floor, there were boxes and pieces of wood thrown about, the wallpaper hung in strips from the damp walls, rotting shutters banged in the wind, hanging from rusted hinges. In fact, the eerie atmosphere of the place forced the three young men to talk in whispers as they went up the stairs. Nicholls went into the small room alone and suddenly, he says, he felt as if something was terribly wrong. His mind and body seemed to have slowed down like a clock which needed winding — it was as if a black shutter had come down over one half of his mind. He staggered back down the stairs and out into the garden, glad of the fresh air on his face as he sank to the grass. He had decided he didn't want any more part in exploring the house.

But St Audries went back. They heard him go upstairs and across the landing. He was whistling. He stopped abruptly — for a moment there was silence. Then Nicholls wrote, 'There was a scream from the house, almost inhuman and yet in Peter's voice, the like of which I hope I shall never hear again, the sort of cry a man who had been stabbed in the back would give.' They heard the sound of a struggle with thuds and screams and as they were about to dash inside again to help him, he ran from the house, his face ashen, his hair and clothes covered in plaster dust. All he could say was, 'The thing . . . it happened . . . out of the room and down the darkness of the corridor something raced . . . it was black, shaped like a man . . . two things I noticed, the first was I could see no face, only blackness. The second was that it made no noise, it raced towards me over that bare floor with no sound . . . suddenly I was knocked flat by an overwhelming force . . . I had this terrible sensation of evil as though I were struggling with something beastly out of hell . . . '

The murderer probably would have made no sound as he chased the terrified girl along a carpeted corridor.

The three young men, now thoroughly frightened and out of their depth, ran to a nearby house for brandy and it was then they were told of the significance of that little room at the top of the stairs.

So I had to see Castel-a-Mare for myself.

In the exact location described, opposite Edwinstowe, there is a gaping hole rather like a missing tooth in an otherwise perfect mouth. A high stone wall runs along the road with a white gate which obviously once led to the back premises of a house. Next door on one side is Norfolk Lodge and Grendon, on the other Monte Rosa where Mr Reburn lives. The big empty patch is his garden where once a three-storey house stood. The gate from the road leads down cement steps, for the garden is well below the level of the road as the cellars of a house would have been — Castel-a-Mare! Mr Reburn said, 'I have often wondered why there is only about a foot of earth over my garden and beneath it seems to be stones and bricks. It is as though a load or two of earth were brought in to try and cover them.'

I wondered what else they might cover. Is it possible the skeleton of a murdered woman does still lie somewhere in that garden? Mr Reburn thinks from various tiles and things he has found on his premises that once they were stables and that from the number of names on the deeds it must have changed hands many times.

No one seems able to answer the question of why the ghost was so evil and if it has left the site. At the moment it seems peaceful and calm, but what would happen if another house were built there?

Going back down the hill, towards the sea, let us go and look at something much more pleasant and harmless, St John's Church, where once during choir practice the organist stopped playing to talk to the boys, and suddenly the instrument started to play itself.

During the 1950s the vicar, the Reverend Anthony Rouse, did a great deal of research on this matter and lectured on his findings. It seems this time the ghost is gentle, being that of a former church organist who died in 1883 — Henry Ditton Newman. He left one of his works incomplete and his ghostly footsteps were heard by many clergy at the house called Montpelier next to the church, as well as his playing on the organ he loved. Outside all is peace, the big gold cross on the tower shining out across the sea . . .

GHOSTS IN PUBS

It is quite extraordinary how many pubs in Devon are reputed to be haunted, nearly always by a monk, who seems on the whole to be benign. But when you think that usually these pubs had been a dwelling for the monks who built the nearby churches, this figures, as the Americans say. However, the first bit of research I did had nothing to do with a monk, neither was it particularly benign, but curious in the extreme.

Some years ago I read a book called *Literary Landmarks of Devon and Cornwall* by R.Thurston Hopkins published in 1926, and a fascinating book it was. The story, which caught my imagination above all and had me haring over to Colyton, was about an evening Mr Hopkins had spent at the Dolphin Inn. After a good meal of cold beef he sat with several of the locals, talking and smoking. Presently a man named Nicholas Apsley joined them, a tall, bearded man of about seventy. He had been a builder and the talk turned to progress, particularly with reference to the car and bus, the way they had given a new lease of life to lonely villages, even bringing business to parts of the country which had been almost dead for 300 years. Then someone said, 'Motors didn't do much good for Bob Levett,' and out came the story of how this man had been run over on the road near Gatcombe Chase. They had carried him into the Dolphin, covered in blood and spattered from head to foot with the paint he had been carrying. He died almost at once and they never found out who had run him over. Someone mentioned the name Plashett; he owned a garage at Musbury and was 'a bit of an inventor'. It seemed he knew more about the accident than he let on. He did say however that a Major Cheyney had driven his big German car into the garage not half an hour after the occurrence. It had a dented wing, spattered with the same colour paint Bob had been carrying.

But nothing was proved, and soon Major Cheyney was killed in the war and young Plashett crashed in an aeroplane. Nicholas said, 'People here don't like talking about it, 'tis all past and done.' Then he paused and added quietly, 'but Bob Levett's been seen since. He waits about on the road between Gatcombe Chase and Colyton where it happened. People hear him running and shouting. They say he's looking for the car that killed him, and he can run like the very devil — no car can shake him off. First of all you hear his feet pattering behind you, pattering in the quiet and the dark, then the hiss of his breath right by you, then he passes you and goes on, out of hearing.' It seems one night a stranger, who knew nothing of the accident or the ghost, knocked up the landlord of the Dolphin, almost speechless with terror. The thing had overtaken him on the road and he was afraid to drive any further.

'They do say sometimes he doesn't pass but springs on the car, and a couple of years ago a car crashed on that very spot and was smashed to bits. The chap driving wasn't killed, but he went mad, kept crying a man was chasing him, going to strangle him. The doctor couldn't pacify him and they found black bruises like finger-marks on his throat. They say that what's been is, and the past can never cease.'

So to Colyton. Things got even curiouser. The oldest local inhabit-ant told me the Dolphin Inn had been a bank for more than 100 years. I had been directed to the place by another local but when I got to the spot the pub was called the Kingfisher, kept by Cherry and Graeme Sutherland, and yet in the passageway at the side was a tiny plaque which read Dolphin House — see what I mean? Everyone in the bar denied ever having heard of this hit and run story and seemed to clam up when I mentioned it.

I drove on to the Ship Inn at Axmouth run by Christopher Chapman, son of Fanny Cradock, where the sea food is superb. They had no ghost and also knew nothing about the Colyton story. There was one customer at the bar who told me he had had a lot of trouble with a TV mast on a cottage roof on his farm. It got the twitch at 8 o'clock every morning, nearly detaching itself from the chimney, although often there was no breath of wind. However they directed me to the Stepps Country Club, about which I had already read in several ghost books. This is said to be an old Priests' Rest House, probably having its origin in the Alien Priory of Axmouth in the reign of Henry II, later converted into a residence for a wealthy merchant in the 1640s. Lola Walton, who owns the club, told me there was

1.   Wistman's Wood

2. Dart Gorge

3. Fernworthy Reservoir

4. & 5.   Warren House Inn — second highest inn in England

6.   St Pancras Church, Widecombe

7. **Tavistock Inn, Poundsgate**
8. **Rock House where Kipling stayed**

9. Norfolk Lodge — one side of the former Castel-a-Mare
10. Monte Rosa — once the stables of Castel-a-Mare

11. Church House Inn, Torbryan

definitely a presence of some kind there; she had felt it herself. Doors opened and closed, taps were found running for no reason. 'When I bought it eight years ago, I was told it was haunted. At the time I said, "You can tell that to the Marines!" but now I've changed my mind. There have been odd happenings. One night I'd closed up and everyone had gone home. I was washing glasses in the bar, when there was a terrific crash upstairs. I heard footsteps and, thinking it might be an intruder, I picked up the poker and crept upstairs. There was nothing, not even the cat! Many people too have felt an intense coldness, even in summer.' There had been a child staying in the house and as she got ready for bed the two doors which enclosed an old fireplace rattled and were pushed outwards as though someone were trying to get out, and yet there wasn't a breath of wind. 'It went on for about ten minutes and terrified me, but perhaps things like that seem to go on longer than they really do. I had my rosary there and I put it round my neck and the thing stopped.'

Mrs Walton showed me a newspaper cutting from the *Seaton News* of 22 March 1974 headed 'Where Things Go Bump In The Night!' It described a recently published book, *Ghosts of Dorset, Devon and Somerset,* and one of the three authors who had combined to write the work was Mary Collier of Musbury. For many years she has been collecting stories of ghostly happenings and the story of Stepps Country Club is told, saying it had the reputation of being haunted for years. A woman who had stayed there in the 1950s said, 'One night at about 11 p.m. I came out of the lavatory to hear the most terrible and unearthly scream, almost inhuman, from just above my head. I told my husband. He's a very down-to-earth person and was extremely sceptical that the screams could be ghostly in origin. However the next night about the same time he himself heard this quite terrible noise and had to admit he was not surprised I had been alarmed. We didn't want to frighten the children and said nothing to anyone, leaving soon after. Then only a week ago I was staying with friends in Mid Devon and some people came to lunch with them. They knew Axmouth and I asked if Stepps was still there, not mentioning our experience, and they said, "Yes, it used to be a smugglers' haunt and had the reputation of being haunted." So then I told them my own experience.'

To return to monks in pubs, I had heard that the Pig and Whistle at Littlehempston kept a chair by the fire reserved for 'Freddie', and that in 1968 when the pub was kept by Marina and Bob Chatterton, she had felt a strange atmosphere always and would not be left by herself. Freddie seems to have been a hunchback monk, possibly French, from Buckfast before the dissolution period. His name most probably was Brother Joseph, and it has been said he rode from the Abbey to meet a local lady of easy virtue, always coming to the same door. This has now been made into a window but does nothing to deter him from entering. The story goes that if anyone approached him likely to tell tales, he would dive into a nearby tunnel leading from the inn to a chapel and would then be found 'telling his beads'.

When I visited the pub I found Mr Thomas and Mr Evans had recently moved in. They said neither of them had actually seen the ghost, but they did admit to a series of quite tragic events which had 'haunted' them. In fact it seemed nothing but bad luck had dogged them — literally. First their much beloved old English sheepdog had been run over right outside the door; then a pedigree retriever, which had seemed in perfect health, had suddenly dropped dead for no apparent reason. 'They are silly things really,' they told me, 'things you couldn't exactly put down to a ghost, but they always happen if one of us has sat in that chair. Bottles explode, not beer, which would be understandable, but blackcurrant juice, and it hadn't even fermented. Some people can definitely feel a cold aura. We have a local, Old Ron. He's a very sensible man, but he can feel a definite presence and sometimes his dog will start to shake and crawl away from Freddie's chair as if he sees something. Our equipment in the cellar has been tampered with — gas pressure systematically turned off by a valve which has to be forcibly turned — the kids couldn't possibly do it. The gas is turned off and the whole of the bottle neck unscrewed. No one else goes down there.'

He went on to tell me they had had workmen in the old cottage next door, one of them an ex-professional boxer, a real down-to-earth type. They used to work all hours to get the job done, then suddenly they refused to work in the evenings. It seems they had been sitting round eating their lunch when one of the carpenters said, 'I've just seen water coming out of that tap.' The others said something like, 'Pull the other one it's got bells on. The tap isn't even connected. There's no water in the pipe to come out of the tap.' It put them off working late in there after that. People have been shoved and pushed from behind and when they've turned round to remonstrate there's just no one there. This is what it usually seems to be, some kind of pressure, a touch, usually at night.

42

Mr Thomas went on, 'One night a fellow sat in "the" chair telling his friends about the ghost, taking the mickey really. Someone said, "You shouldn't do that," but he took no notice. They left and went 200 yards up the road and hit the bank; the car was a write off. They say if you do actually see the ghost there'll be a death in the family. Well, thank heaven none of us have actually seen it, but we've still lost our dogs and we've come to the conclusion that although he may be benign, as a monk in his day he was bad and his spirit now is uneasy. To start with we just took the mickey out of the idea, but now, with all these things happening . . .'

There is a well, now enclosed, but somehow this added to the feeling of unease. Although it has a lid, it is 45 feet deep and the water has been known to rise within a short distance of the top in wet weather.

Dennis Hawke runs the Church House Inn at Torbryan. Years ago this village was on the main stageroute to Plymouth, one of the largest and most important parishes in Devon. The Inn was built in 1400 to house the workmen engaged on restoring the church which dates back to the eighth century. Beer was brewed on the premises, and the oven of the old bakehouse can still be seen, as was once the ghost by the local policeman! He was new to the district, and anxious to get to know the locals, he asked who the old fellow in the corner was. The landlord could see no one. An RAF member who slept by the fire in the bar because the pub was full, also saw a monk-like figure which walked straight through the wall. In 1960 David Bassett, the then landlord, heard footsteps and said, 'Maybe it was Henry VIII who was reputed to have stayed here on his way to visit the Petre family at Tor Newton House.' In 1968 Mick Heap ran the pub and his dog stood with its hackles rising one night, staring into an empty corner and from then on would bark at the same time each night. When I asked the present barman if he had had any odd experiences he said he had felt a sudden coldness in a room in which a huge fire burned, and added, rather ruefully, 'I bought a good-luck pixie from a gypsy and immediately after I fell down the stairs, broke my tooth on a toffee and burnt my hand in the fire, so I threw the pixie away and cursed it. I'm glad to say ever since I've been OK, so maybe the ghost didn't like gypsies or pixies.'

The Monk's Retreat at Broadhempston is also haunted, but by nothing more alarming than a perfume of incense and flowers, which always seems to be strongest at the time of church festivals. In 1968

Fred Matthews, the landlord, found it a very restful atmosphere with nothing out of the way to report other than a spiral staircase which had been found hidden behind a fireplace. Bickleigh Mill at Stoneycombe has a new landlord who is Dutch and as he had only just taken over hadn't had much time to encounter the ghost! But Mrs Toffolo who lives in a caravan on the car park said she had seen the ghost of the miller in the kitchen.

At the Old Inn at Widecombe a child is heard sobbing pitifully and during 1968 Geoff Ellis and his wife who often encountered this sound, wondered if it had anything to do with the suicide of the girl buried at nearby Jay's Grave. There's also 'Harry' who seems harmless enough, simply wandering now and then into the bar!

The Bishop Lacey at Chudleigh was the only building left standing whole after the terrible fire of 1807, but in the fourteenth century Bishop Edmund Lacey chose this for his summer vacation, much as Archbishop Ramsey still does the inn at Holne, except Lacey actually stayed at the monastery, parts of which can still be seen. The Inn itself is said to be haunted by a cloaked figure which some years ago the landlord saw as he was clearing the bar at closing time. He pointed this out to the visitor. However the man took no notice and started up the stairs. The landlord shouted at him and then followed him, only to meet his wife coming down. No one had passed her.

At the Royal Castle Hotel at Dartmouth a ghostly coach still haunts the hall. It is probable that the first building on this site was much older even than the date of 1639 over the door, this possibly being when it was reconstructed. But it seems Princess Mary of Orange didn't like the sea and so chose to come to Dartmouth in the best weather possible without waiting for her husband William, who intended to follow immediately with his army. Bad weather however made him land at Brixham instead and he sent a horseman to Dartmouth to tell his wife and ask her to be ready for the coach to take her and her ladies to join him. The coach arrived hot on the heels of the messenger at 2 in the morning, and still does so, preceded by the galloping messenger. However what was once the yard is now the hall and many people have heard the rumble of wheels over cobbles, the clatter of hooves, doors opening and slamming, but no one seems to be able to explain exactly why this haunting takes place, and certainly there is nothing sinister about it.

Coombe Cellars on the Teign was once the haunt of smugglers. In 1968 Margaret Marshall, the barmaid, woke every night with the terrible feeling she was being strangled and was convinced the room was haunted. So bad was this that she had to have sleeping pills from the doctor. No one really took her seriously, but then a most incredible coincidence occurred. Jim Harvey, the proprietor, went to a sale and bought some old pictures, among them a painting of a woman being murdered 100 years earlier by a burglar who had broken into her bedroom. The room was the one the barmaid now occupied.

Finally a town ghost living in the cellars of the Prince Regent Hotel in Paignton. It seems he was a harmless enough fellow for the two children who lived in the pub with their parents made him Christmas cards and left them on the cellar steps. The ghost was said to be called Alfred and came from Shepton Mallet where he had been hanged at the age of 34 during the Napoleonic wars, but I could not verify this information. It seems he used to live in a brick tower on the site but when this was pulled down he moved into the pub cellar and has been known to switch on the record player, turn off lights and interfere with the gas pressure in the cellar which controls the beer, a quite common occurrence with these ghosts in pubs. Maybe the modern 'gassing' of beers annoys these fellows from the past, and who could blame them. The landlord said, 'I think he messes around with the gas to draw attention to himself, he's lonely, he likes company and he knows someone has to go down and fix it — but I must say I wish he'd leave us alone when we're busy in the summer — I get so exasperated sometimes I shout at him.'

MORE GHOSTS

My cousin, just home from South Africa, heard me say I'd been to Berry Pomeroy. She commiserated thinking I meant to the interment of a beloved dog. I explained it was the castle to which I referred, perhaps one of the most romantic and most haunted castles in all Devon as it has two buildings, one within the other. Almost all the remains of the very large fortified castle date from 1300, but it was certainly not the first building to stand here. It takes its name from the Pomeroy family who came from France, and it was sold to the Seymour family for £4,000 in 1548. Edward Seymour lived in the mansion standing within the castle. However this is not a history book, and it is the ghost stories and legends attached to the area in which we are interested.

It seems two sisters, Eleanor and Margaret de Pomeroy were in love with the same man. The former, who was mistress of the castle, was jealous of her younger and more beautiful sister, so she shut her up in the dungeon and starved her to death, and it is her ghost which on certain nights walks along the ramparts.

Reports of this haunting go back many years but they were brought into prominence when a certain eminent doctor, Sir Walter Farquhar, wrote about it in his memoirs. He had been called to attend the wife of the steward of the castle. As he waited in the parlour the door opened and a young lady, evidently in great distress, passed him and went up the small staircase, giving no reply to his enquiries if he could help her. However his patient was very ill and for the moment he forgot the incident.

Some days later he recalled it and asked the steward who the young lady was. The man's face was ashen as he said, 'Now I know my wife will die!' 'Nonsense,' said the doctor. 'She has passed the crisis and is well on the road to recovery. In fact in a few days she will be up and about.' The husband was unconvinced. During that night the doctor received a message telling him his patient had died.

It is said Lady Margaret stands on the ruins of the staircase beckoning to the unwary visitor and between her and her victim is a chasm where the staircase has collapsed. Into this he will fall to his death.

Near the gateway are the ruins of an old pleasance and an ancient arbour. Here one of the daughters of the house used to meet her love, who, like Romeo, was an enemy of her family. The girl's brother, coming upon the lovers, slew him with his sword. Now inside the castle entrance, when the summer moon is full, the shadowy figures of the young lovers stretch out to meet each other's arms. but never do because of the Pomeroy hatred which keeps them apart.

To reach the castle you follow the long drive through beech trees, silver birch and rhododendrons, and the atmosphere of history all about you is so strong that it wouldn't be surprising to see a gaily caprisoned knight canter across the meadow beside the stream which tumbles through the gorge below the castle.

After the rebellion in 1549 when the order went out for castles to be destroyed, two young Pomeroy knights refused to destroy their beloved home. Somewhere in the grounds they buried their treasure, blindfolded their horses, and then spurred them over the cliff to death in the valley below, choosing rather to die free than become defeated.

Many people to whom I have talked about Berry Pomeroy have remarked on the sense of evil, loneliness and desolation that haunts the area. Photographs have shown shadowy figures, and in 1968 a woman took her two children aged seven and nine for a picnic thinking they would enjoy playing and romping among the ruins. All they did was beg to be taken home, refusing to leave her side. Does something of the violent past indeed remain to be picked up by some people, specially the young, waves from the past imprinted on the atmosphere, recalling the happenings?

Edna White of Torquay told me of friends who had walked up to the castle from below, passing cottages that were derelict, seeing people in rags, ruined barns, and felt this extraordinary air of absolute evil. In fact one of the party was so upset by it she turned back to the car, the others went on through scenes of utter neglect.

Several days later, fascinated by what they had seen, they returned. They simply couldn't believe their eyes. There had been a complete transformation. The cottages were beautifully restored and painted, gardens well tended, barns roofed and full of sacks of corn, all they could imagine was that originally they had gone back in time, had a vision of the past. It had been on a hot, still day. Could it have been some kind of mirage?

Recently a reporter saw two photographs taken by holidaymakers showing shadowy outlines of a man and woman taken on different days by people totally unknown to each other. The one showing the outlines of a man was examined by the Psychic Research Society who confirmed it was a ghostly image. Both of these were by the ruined entrance to Margaret's tower. Mr Wilsman, the curator, said 'Some very down-to-earth and sensible people have seen many odd things.'

Winifred Fairchild of Torquay told me, 'In the summer of 1932 my sister came to Torquay on holiday, and as both of us were interested in old Devon buildings, we decided to visit Berry Pomeroy castle. The afternoon was very hot and still and after looking round the ruins we sat on the wall to rest. All was pleasant for some time and then I began to feel uneasy, as though someone were watching me. I expected any moment to feel a hand touch me. At last I looked round. Nothing there of course, but I still felt a chilling presence. At that time I knew nothing of any stories connected with the castle. To my relief my sister suggested we walk on. After we left the spot well behind us she surprised me by remarking, "I didn't like that place. I felt I was being watched." ' Note — it was a very hot still day again.

When I went there recently the Department of the Environment, who now have an interest in the site, had people digging and replacing stones which had fallen from the top of the building. One man told me he had leaned down to pat a dog no one else could see, another told me that ley lines crossed the site and he himself felt a kind of electrical magic there, but one of the girls said she found nothing eerie about it, rather the reverse, it seemed a happy place.

And now to a very different site — Hendham House in the beautiful South Hams area of Devon. Unfortunately its history is not recorded, the only date available being 1779 on one of the walls, but Robert Hatch who lives there told me he had often heard footsteps when he was totally alone in the house. He added: 'A friend who had been in the RAF with me, a very prosaic sort of chap, was staying here. He went upstairs for something and when he came down he was quite annoyed and asked me why I had followed him. I said, "Now don't you start!" I hadn't moved from the chair I was sitting in.' He went on: 'We heard glasses tinkling, no voices, just glasses, and threw open the door, but of course nothing. One day my cat, Prince, stood looking up the stairs as if watching someone come down. As I went to follow him it was as if I was pushed back by a tangible force, and then I heard the rustle of skirts.'

A friend of his who was a medium went over the house. She said, 'I want to talk to you about Sarah. She is trying to communicate with you, and if you don't let her then she will always haunt this place, because she wants people to know William didn't do it.' She could give him no more information, only that the girl is called Sarah Mountford. Oddly enough, soon after, an old lady of 89 came and asked if she might see inside the house where she had lived eighty years ago. It was she who then mentioned a murder in one of the bedrooms, and Colin Wilson has been to the house and discussed the strange occurrences with him. 'He said it was well known that an influence could remain and that if Sarah was waiting to be "liberated" she might think I am a sensitive person to whom she can get across the fact that William did not do this murder. The deeds to the house are lost, but through research it has been discovered that once a William Gayle lived here in about 1857. So this could be the William for whom poor Sarah seeks, calling his name on the stairs and sobbing.'

There are other unhappy ladies not too far away, the Grey Lady of Dartington Hall who has been wandering about for the last 200 years or more, but the Champernowne family themselves have always been a little sceptical about this. Of course there have, over the years, been tales of horror, murder and suicide in a house of this age. A nannie saw the lady of the house bending over a child's cot when actually she was miles away and the apparition frightened the poor girl out of her wits. In October 1712 Elizabeth Champernowne was ill and being cared for by a nurse who got drunk, and her patient with a high fever, wandered outside and was found dead in the snow. There was the wife of Arthur Champernowne who was pushed down the stairs in 1766 after quarrelling with her husband. Maybe these ladies do return.

There are tales of the hauntings of the White Lady of Buckfast whose husband was killed by the poisoned dagger of a man who had been a rival for her hand in marriage, but the murderer himself was so badly injured in the fight that he too died and Lady Dyonisia, the object of his affection, involved in the brawl, was killed and she remains to wander and haunt the grave of her killer in the Abbey Churchyard.

Among the many flesh and blood ladies to whom I am indebted for material is Emily Clay of Brixham who worked like a beaver to bring me reports of hauntings, some of which we ran to ground, some of which we never found. We met many people, some of whom wished to remain anonymous, others kindly allowing their names to be mentioned. Among these was Mrs Barker who had once rented part of a house known as Friar's Pardon in Brixham. This building was at one time a monastery when the white friars were sent to build St Mary's church, but the ghost who is said to haunt the building is Charles who committed suicide. He had been given the property, when the monasteries were dissolved, for services rendered and turned it into a Manor House. He was the Lord of the Manor, but his son fell in love with a totally unsuitable girl, from both families' point of view, and her father forced her to marry someone else of her own kind. When the boy found out he tried to stop the wedding but couldn't. His horse returned home without him and Charles found him hanged. He became so distraught himself that he returned home and killed himself. It is the clatter of the horse's hooves which can be heard on the cobblestones as it returns without its rider to the back of the house — except that now there are no cobblestones.

Mrs Barker told me she lived in the house about sixteen years ago for several months. 'None of us would stay in the house alone, and each time my brother came home from college he said how he hated the house — not that the ghost is in the least malignant, more mischievous, locking people in bathrooms and so on. During the war lights were seen in the house and the police were called in, although there was no one there and no electricity or gas either.' She told me she and her husband are Roman Catholics and their priest himself had been to the house and said there was no reason why there should not be a spirit of some kind there. 'In fact,' she added, 'one priest used to say "Good night Charlie" when he left!' It seems a Mrs Dyke from New Zealand visited Mrs Barker, but would not cross the threshold into the house although no one had told her previously of the ghost.

Mrs Barker ended by saying 'My husband was a total unbeliever, but he too felt the atmosphere in the house - not evil, just a presence, definitely not a poltergeist of any kind.' She paused and as I got to the door to leave she said, 'the extraordinary part is that every time this story gets written about the notes disappear! Years ago someone for the *Herald Express* was writing a book about it and everything just disappeared, so it intrigued me when I heard you were going to do it. I wondered what would happen.' Laughing, I showed her the tape recorder I had used for the interview.

I didn't laugh when I got home and found the tape with that particular section was blank. The other interviews on the same cassette were perfectly normal!

The Milton Street area seems to suffer particularly from various ghosts. Mrs Beer said several people had seen a little old lady in black in her house, including a Mrs Fitch who described her as grey-haired with a bun, wearing a floor-length black dress and a shawl with a white apron. She seemed to walk quite normally, not glide like ghosts are meant to, neither was she transparent. Another lady who has an old cottage which once belonged to a sea captain said, 'One lovely summer evening I was walking up the stairs in the old part of the house and I heard someone walking behind me with a heavy tread like sea boots would make. I thought it was my son home early, teasing me, but when I turned round there was no one there. The strange part was that when I stopped, the footsteps went on and passed me sounding as if they were on bare boards although the stairs are thickly carpeted.'

At the foot of Temperance Steps on King Street stands Coffin House, said to be built in the shape of a coffin by a man for his daughter since he disliked the man she wanted to marry! It isn't just these days that such bitter parental discord occurs.

Finally we visited the Three Elms pub in Drew Street and talked to the son of the landlord who told us their ghost is an old man who had shot himself when the house was a farm about 100 years ago, explaining that parts of the building go back more than 400 years.

'I have heard footsteps, so had the previous landlord, and Mrs Thompson, our cleaning lady, said she definitely saw a ghost in the pink room. When I was twelve I heard someone coming up the stairs in the middle of the night. At first I thought it was my grandfather, but he had a wooden leg and this person hadn't. I flew into my parents' room in a terrible state. Another time my father heard the most indescribable and terrifying scream and thought it was my baby sister, but when he rushed into her room she was fast asleep. Sometimes the dog won't go upstairs, and one night Mum was in the bath, when she heard someone banging on the door which made her very angry, specially when they wouldn't answer. She came down and asked us who'd been messing about. We told her we'd all been together in the sitting room. We're not a family to imagine things. We've always lived in new houses before and never thought about ghosts, but my father was really scared and he's the last person to believe in such things.' He hesitated a moment and then he said, 'There's no doubt it's a very creepy place at night and I have to admit I wouldn't stay here on my own.'

POLTERGEISTS
AND TRAVELLING GHOSTS

Reports of poltergeists seem fairly common in the South West. I read of one said to pester the inmates of a big Victorian house set back in its own grounds near the roundabout approaching Exeter from the Ottery side, even making life intolerable for the troops billetted there during the war, but I couldn't trace it. However, I did find several people who could talk to me about Albert, the poltergeist once said to haunt Aller House near Newton Abbot.

Mrs Mills lived in the nearby farm for sixty years. 'I often called there, it was a solidly built house with big rooms and a greenhouse, I remember. I never heard anything myself but of course there was a lot of talk about it, mostly when it was turned into flats. One lot of people there were the Powlings.'

I wrote to Max Powling. He told me he was afraid his evidence was negative. 'I lived there from the age of nine till I was twenty-two and was sublimely unaware of anything other than a normal home between the years 1925 and 1937.' But it seems before the Powlings moved in the house had been empty for some years. Previously it had belonged to the Devon Hide, Skin and Manure Company and it was their manager, Albert Victor Judd, who committed suicide there.

During the war the Council put evacuees in, and then Mr Weaver bought it. Mrs Weaver told me, 'It was when we were first married we lived there. It was a big house and we made it into flats. It was old and inconvenient with no hot water or anything like that, but the hauntings were after my time, and of course it was pulled down. All that's left is one wall with an old chimney and a fireplace.'

But there had been those who had felt the presence of something. It switched off the radio and made itself felt to John Durston and his wife Carol who moved into one of the flats on 31 August 1963. Furniture and crockery were broken, and the local parson, the Reverend Gordon Langford himself said he could feel an evil atmosphere in the house when they had called on him for advice. In fact it got so bad that on 10 November 1963 the Bishop of Exeter, Dr Robert Mortimore, took a service which lasted for 35 minutes and included the sprinkling of Holy Water. Some people said they had seen the apparition watching the proceedings.

On 8 December 1963 the *News of the World* reported fresh trouble in the flat next door occupied by Mr Leonard Culley. He was sitting doing some work when he suddenly felt a terrible coldness and looking over his shoulder he met the gaze of a man of about forty dressed in Edwardian fashion. He jumped to his feet and the apparition faded. It was at the end of the 1960s that the house was demolished and replaced by the storage buildings of Unigate Foods.

But exorcism should be kept in its true perspective, for it is more than likely that the root of the trouble lies within people and not places. It is not always easy to accept this, as 'Penny' of Paignton, who wishes to remain anonymous, told me in relating her own experience.

Shortly after moving into a council flat she noticed an extraordinary coldness and at night she heard someone who seemed to be sorting through papers. Her daughter too was kept awake, although at first they didn't tell each other of this fact. When they did, they decided it must be noisy neighbours and tried all the usual methods of noise exclusion such as ear plugs, but then Penny saw a figure dressed in a black cloak over a white dress, and her grandson also saw 'this lady'. However worse was to come. Quite suddenly her daughter underwent a complete change of personality, including dyeing her hair a ghastly shade of red. Eventually in desperation Penny asked a medium for help, who told her a girl had lived on the spot at one time, probably in the 1800s. She had been attacked and killed and was now an earth-borne spirit. She was young and had red hair...

At her request Penny and her daughter were found alternative accommodation. The medium explained that probably the visitations had occurred to them particularly because originally the accommodation had been used by elderly and retired people. She thought it was because Penny's daughter was young and the girl was seeking someone her own age and had therefore manifested herself in this manner.

An even more vicious poltergeist was reported at Sampford Peverell in 1810 when a family called Chave lived in a house where not only the usual sounds and breakages of china occurred, but also the maids were violently attacked as they lay in bed. Once again the local clergyman took up the cause of the tenant of the house and wrote to the *Taunton Courier* on 18 August saying he was utterly unable to account for any of the phenomena, even swearing an oath to this effect before the Master in Chancery at Tiverton. The floorboards were said to vibrate so violently that dust rose, ceilings shook, pictures fell from the wall and so on. However Mr Marriott, the editor of the paper, prompted by the owner of the house, Mr Tally, produced a pamphlet saying the whole thing was engineered by the servants banging on the ceilings with mops and that the hauntings were all a fabrication by Mr Chave who wished to get his own back on the landlord for a quarrel over the rent, and thus depreciate the value of the house. Mr Baring Gould in his account agrees in principal with this view, but there was another explanation. The house was found years later to have double walls with a passage between and smugglers had used it for the hiding of contraband. It was suggested they made the disturbances to keep people away! This explanation is often given for similar hauntings in the old days. For instance, at Chambercombe Manor, Ilfracombe, smugglers were said to be responsible for the haunting of a room whose existence even had been unknown till 1865 when the owner realised there were more windows than rooms in his house! When the room was discovered, inside were found remains of a tapestry and carved black furniture falling to pieces, also the grinning skull and skeleton said to be of a Spanish woman shipwrecked at Hele and captured by smugglers. The room can still be seen through a hole in the wooden partition of the staircase.

As well as what one might call these static ghosts are the travelling ones. In the summer of 1962 a motorist driving from Modbury to Gara Bridge saw an old dark blue or black Daimler laundalette of the early 1920s with a wire netting roof rack, but when he rounded the bend it had vanished. A week later he saw it again. Altogether he saw it on three occasions and when eventually he mentioned it he found it was well known locally. The driver wore a peaked cap and dark jacket in the style of an old fashioned chauffeur, but no one had ever seen his face. I could find no particular story or legend to account for this, the only odd thing being, once again, as with so many other phenomena, it is usually seen on a warm summer evening.

The late Syd Wills told me about the lady who used to haunt the bridge at Stover. One night in 1961 a lady was riding her bike home from a WI meeting. She reached the stone bridge over the river Bovey near Stover, when she realised someone 'surrounded by a kind of fluorescent glow' was running along beside her. It waved its arms and tried to jump in front of her. When she got home, her son, seeing how upset she was, went out on his motor bike to investigate and he had the same experience. The only explanation I can give is that it is said all old bridges are haunted because of the human sacrifices made on the original sites to placate the river gods who disliked their domain being invaded. Nearby Stover House itself is said to be haunted. In the time of the Templers it was difficult to keep maids, and in fact one of the pupils I know, who used to go there to school, told me the dormitories are still haunted.

Syd also told me about nearby Lindridge House, burned down in 1963. It was once owned by Leofric, Bishop of Exeter, and then after the Dissolution in 1539 it became Crown Property. It changed hands many times until in 1770 John Line bought it. However he only lived another seven years and his widow married John Templer who succeeded the Reverend Gilbert Yarde as rector of Teigngrace. Yarde was battered to death by his former gardener, John Greenslade, the man having asked for a reference on changing his job. Yarde gave him one in Latin. On applying for various jobs Greenslade noticed prospective employers seemed to change their tune directly they read the reference! He got it translated. It read: 'Gone from me, and fit for no man.' When he found out he killed the rector, stealing his money and gold watch. For some time he got away with it, but one night in his cups he showed the watch to a mate. He was tried and found guilty and on 18 August 1783 hanged on the gibbet at Little Haldon near Lindridge, his ghost still wandering the area.

Of course there are many phantom hitchhikers, and possibly with the horrific motorway murders more will appear. The A38 has its own particular haunt, reported in the *Western Morning News* in August 1970. Although not actually entirely in Devon, it is so close it bears the telling. The ten mile stretch centred on Wellington in Somerset is said to be the haunt of a phantom with a torch, a middle-aged man in a long grey macintosh who stands in the middle of the road near Heatherton Grange Hotel. He has also appeared at White Ball causing a motor cyclist to fall from his machine in terror.

There was a letter in the *Express and Echo* from a lorry driver,

12.   The Author — Judy Chard

13. The Monk's Retreat, Broadhempston

14.   St John's Church and Montpelier House

15. Coombe Cellars on the Teign

16.   Royal Castle, Dartmouth

17. & 18. Berry Pomeroy

19. **Buckfast Abbey**
20. **Dartington Hall**

21. Hendham House
22. Cabell's Tomb

Mr Harold Unsworth, describing how he had been driving back to his depot at Cullompton and this man stopped him for a lift. The weather was terrible and the man seemed to be drenched to the skin, so although it was against his usual policy he stopped. The man asked to be dropped at the old Beam Bridge at Holcombe. His conversation consisted entirely of details of all the terrible fatal accidents which had occurred near the bridge.

The same thing happened three times to this driver on this journey, and then there was a gap of some years until the apparition appeared again. This time when they stopped at the bridge, he asked the driver to wait while he picked up some cases. He didn't reappear and the driver went without him, only to see him again some miles further up the road, waving his torch. He swerved to avoid him, but the man seemed literally to throw himself under his wheels. He jammed on his brakes and the articulated lorry jack-knifed, but fortunately not out of control. The figure was still in the middle of the road, shaking his fist, but this time as Mr Unsworth approached it disappeared.Could it be, like the man at Colyton, this was one of the many motorists or pedestrians killed on this road and doomed forever to hitchhike?

In 1970 Mrs Kathy Swithenbank, driving from Oake, also saw the same ghost, but did not stop. All this gained interest when I read in the *Sunday Express* in April 1979 of the experience of Mrs Babs Davidson who was driving home in the winter moonlight on a well known road near her home, when suddenly the way ahead was no longer familiar. Part of the road was blacked out, a road she had never seen before forked mistily away to her right. It seems nine people had died on that piece of carriageway in Kent since November 1977.

But the most famous local legend to do with highways in Devon must be the one of the Hairy Hands for which there seems to be no explanation. Is there some kind of reserve of psychic power in the area, is it simply a manifestation of force? There doesn't seem to be any mention of it before the second decade of the present century. Perhaps it is the presence of some malignant influence, disembodied matter neither of the human nor of the Spirit world but earthbound between the two, freed from the body but not from the scene of some crime committed during life. Perhaps violent death and emotions can leave imprints on the ether concentrated with such force as to form definite emanations. Is this more ridiculous than a TV personality appearing to a prehistoric man out of a box?

I was only once frightened here myself, in the Archerton area, when I got enveloped in a Dartmoor mist, thick and obliterating, so that I suddenly felt isolated in time. Perhaps it was the utter silence after the noise we live in. After all there is a very narrow margin between loneliness and plain fear. Who can say? I only know I'm inclined to avoid the area.

The odd happenings here between Post Bridge and Two Bridges became of interest to the general public in the early 1920s. In 1921 there were three motoring accidents near the gate of Archerton Drive on Nine Mile Hill and the *Daily Mail* of 14 and 15 October 1921 reported these. The first occurrence was in March 1921. Dr Helby, the prison doctor at Princetown, was riding a bike with a sidecar containing two children. The engine literally detached itself from the machine — there was no other way of describing it. The children jumped clear, but he was killed.

A few weeks later a motor coach mounted the bank on the Lakehead side of the road and one woman was badly hurt: The driver said, 'I felt hands pull the wheel towards Lakehead,' but no one listened to him.

On a dull, foggy Friday, 26 August, an Army officer was riding a motor bike and was thrown on the verge at the same place, suffering shock and scratches. He was a very experienced rider, and he said, 'It just wasn't my fault. Something seemed to drive me off the road and a pair of hairy hands closed over mine. I tried to fight them but they were too strong.'

As these stories gained importance the *Daily Mail* sent investigators to the spot and eventually roadmen altered the camber of the road, for it is true that many moorland roads do have a slope which can give the feeling of being pulled downwards, but these vehicles turned upwards towards the Lakehead side, and the bus and officer's cycle were both travelling uphill.

In 1923 a moorman said he heard a terrible scream in the area and felt a cold blast of air come from Archerton gate. In 1924 a woman and her husband parked their caravan half a mile from the road a mile west of Nine Mile Hill. In the night she woke with a feeling of impending danger. Then she screamed. An enormous pair of hairy hands were clawing at the window. She said, 'I knew the hands were not of any human and somehow they wished us ill. I made the sign of the cross and prayed to God for our safety. They vanished . . .'

In 1961 a man was driving from Plymouth to Chagford. His car overturned and he was found to be dead beneath it. The experts who examined both the vehicle and the body could find no logical explanation for the accident which had occurred in exactly the same spot as the others.

Of equal fame is the story of Jan Coo, the apprentice at Rowbrook farm who was pixie-led. One evening as he returned from hoeing turnips near the river he burst into the farm kitchen where his companions were already waiting for their supper, sitting round the open hearth. He told them between gasps for breath that he had heard a voice crying in great distress down by the river. They rushed to the door to listen. At first no one could hear anything. Then suddenly a voice out of the darkness called quite clearly, 'Jan Coo! Jan Coo!' At once they got their lanterns and ran to the river bank to search, thinking someone might be in trouble in the swiftly flowing Dart. They found nothing. The next night the voice came again. This time they answered it. The call ceased at once. But night after night all through that winter it called 'Jan Coo! Jan Coo!' In early spring it ceased. Then one summer evening as Jan and another labourer plodded up the hill from work, they heard it cry again. This time it came from the other side of the river, from Langamarsh Pit, which of course everyone knew was haunted by pixies.

Jan turned and ran towards the voice like someone possessed. His companion stood stunned, watching him go and cross the river on some boulders. The voice still called and now darkness began to fill the valley. He could no longer see Jan Coo, all he heard was the brawling noise of the river over the stones. He rushed into the farm kitchen shouting to everyone to come and help. Once more they went down to the river with lanterns. They searched and called all night. They found no one — nothing.

The voice was never heard again and neither was Jan Coo ever found. Maybe some pixie, enamoured by his charms, had lured him away to live with her forever in her palace under Langamarsh Pit. Some people say it was simply a wood pigeon they heard calling. If Jan had been drowned his body would have been found — it never was.

Being as curious as Kipling's elephant's child, I went to see Algy May who has lived at Rowbrook since 1953. His mild blue eyes looked at me with amusement when I asked if he believed Jan Coo had been pixie-led. He drew back the kitchen curtain and pointed out across the valley. 'The stepping stones are behind the island leading across to Langamarsh Pit. If you hear the river make a particular sound over the boulders, people say it means someone is going to die.' Then he pointed to the old longhouse which still stands beside the more modern farmhouse, itself 100 years old. 'That's where Jan Coo lived as an apprentice. At one time the French family lived there, and a curious story is told by Hermon French about them. His father was in bed in that room you can see with the open window, three boys in the bed which was often the way with big families. I suppose they were in their early teens. Their father was up in the field hoeing turnips and he saw a terrific flash, a fireball down on the farm. He rushed down to find the lightning had gone right through the house and killed the boy sleeping in the middle of the bed. Hermon's father on one side and his uncle the other were unscathed. The one in the middle burnt to death.'

He told me too about Samuel Hannaford who lived across the moor at Round Hill near Hexworthy. One day in 1826 he'd ridden across the moor to Brent Fair. 'Often done it myself' Algy said. 'He had a skinful of cider and as the effects wore off on the way home, he realised he wasn't riding his own horse. Fact was he'd got mixed up with some gipsies and they said, ''We got a better horse than that of yours, we'll swop.'' Of course it wasn't better, for his had been a first class animal.' He paused and pointed out of the window again, 'Can't quite see it from here, but down there's Hangman's Pit. When he got there I imagine he thought, ''My God, I can't face my wife having got the worst of the bargain'', and he just hanged him-self. He used the new halter that the gipsies had put on the horse they swopped.' Algy chuckled: 'Now comes the really interesting part of the story. Norman Perryman of Stoke Farm told me his father — might have been his grandfather — was coming from the Fair too a bit later, passing Hangman's, and he saw this fellow hanging from the tree on this new halter and said ''Oh that's a waste of a good halter!'' so he pinched it. No one else has ever mentioned this, only Norman, but I think it's the best part of the whole story!'

Algy couldn't tell me what happened after Mr Perryman had cut Samuel down, but I wondered if he'd known the old Devon legend that to possess a rope by which a person has been hanged ensures good luck! Before I left I asked him if he had any theory of what really happened to Jan Coo back in the 1800s. He laughed, 'No, but maybe he wasn't happy here. I think he just ran off. It all happened in the early summer and some people say when the river is a certain height you can still hear the sound "Jan Coo!" but you have to remember in the old story there's quite a lot of poetic licence. For a start it says "they opened the kitchen door and looked down the river." Well you can't see it from here. But in those days they did cultivate the land right down to Eagle Rock — you can see the old workings — and there's no doubt he would have been coming up with the other young apprentices after a day's work in the fields. I think it's just a legend.'

But there are other sounds too on the moor which fill some people with horror. The Chaw Gulley Raven, said to be one of the pair Noah took into the ark, sits above the old mine near the Princetown to Moretonhampstead road at Chaw Gully, warning people who try to find the gold said to be hidden in the mine not to lower themselves into its depth. Those who have done so, when suspended on a rope to a certain depth, have been seized by a hand coming from the side of the shaft, cased with a stonelike wall, and the rope has been cut. Next day the body is found laid out on the heather at the top of the mine.

Another bird sound of disaster is that of a robin if he enters a house and shows no desire to leave but sits calling 'weep weep', a sure presage of death.

Miss Theo Brown in the *Transactions of the Devonshire Association* in 1958 tells the story of the Bleeding Hawk of Hillersdon, the property of Mr Patrick Grant Sturgis. This mummified hawk is said to ooze blood whenever England is about to be at war and to continue to do so till the emergency is past. It was brought to Hillersdon near Cullompton in 1887 by the explorer W.J.A.Grant, who acquired it in Egypt, where it was said to have been found in the tomb of a sister of Tutankhamen. Mr Grant had a notable career and on one occasion when he and his companions were starving in some remote place, it is said they drew lots and ate one of their number! He died at Hillersdon in 1935. In 1924 he had told a press reporter that the hawk had begun to bleed just before the Boer War, ceasing just before the treaty was signed, and remained dry as dust until ten days before the outbreak of the Great War, oozing blood until the Armistice was signed. The late Lord Baden Powell witnessed this phenomenon and it is said he was much impressed by it.

Mr Greig sends a story dated 3 December 1957. It happened when living near Holsworthy he saw a great ghost cat with eyes as big as saucers which used to sit on top of a stone gatepost near Morwenstowe. A man there said he wasn't afraid of no ghost, and hit it with a stick. The cat jumped on his back and clung there while he ran home. Ever after he was bowed down as if with a great weight on his back — which proves the truth of the story. I am indebted to the historian from Ipplepen, Mr Honeywill, for those tales being brought to my notice.

On Midsummer Eve the forty grey wethers on Sittaford Tor turn back into sheep and graze till dawn on the slopes of the Tor. If you can catch and shear one before it turns back into stone, you can make a fortune, but you also have to get a cup of dew from the top of Kestor, the work being done with the shears of a dead man, buried with him, and dug up and dipped into the river at Teignhead before starting!

I suppose the White Bird of the Oxenhams is the most famous 'feathered' haunt. This bird appeared again and again down the years, fluttering over the heads of any member of the family about to die, an ancient family of considerable importance and influence who lived near Okehampton.

Of the numerous reports of its appearance, perhaps the most interesting is of its visit to Sir James Oxenham on the eve of his daughter Margaret's wedding. The full text of the poem telling this story can be seen in the *Transactions of the Devonshire Association* in 1896 sent in by Miss E.Gibbs of South Tawton, who copied it from the Housekeeper's Commonplace Book at Oxenham House.

Margaret was Sir James's only daughter and heiress. She had been courted by Bertram who was unfortunate enough to receive a blow on the head which sent him mad; however eventually Margaret recovered from her sorrow and fell in love with a knight by the name of John. It was on the eve of the wedding at Zeal Monachorum when Sir James saw the 'silvery breasted bird'. Just as the wedding service was about to start Margaret gave a blood curdling scream and a crimson stain flowed down her white satin dress from a dagger wound in her heart. The mad Bertram had thrust it there, and then plunged it into his own breast with a 'maniacal laugh'.

Three members of the family died in 1635 and at each death the white bird appeared. In the eighteenth century William Oxenham saw the bird in his room and within a few days was dead. In Kensington in 1873 workmen erecting some scaffolding on a house opposite where a member of the family lay ill, watched as a white bird made repeated attempts to enter the bedroom. Shortly after they heard the occupant had died. Just before the first world war, Amyas Oxenham died after a white bird flew into his room at Barnfield Crescent in Exeter. His son, the last of the Oxenhams, died in Canada and the family is now extinct. In 1976 it was reported in the *Western Morning News* that the thirteenth century Oxenham Manor at South Tawton had been restored to its former elegance by Dr Nigel Lycett who had made it into a centre of healing and that Mrs Lycett planned to put paid to the story of the white bird by keeping white doves!

Another white bird story, given to me in confidence, the teller wishing to remain anonymous, concerns Laughter Hole Farm. I quote it as I received it: 'Laughter Hole Farm lies on the track between Dunnabridge Pound and Bellever, now a smallholding with a modern bungalow in the Forestry Commission plantation. In the eighteenth century it was a larger farm, the house, now a farm building, against the track. A farmer and his daughter lived there, the mother having died and the other children dispersed. The daughter was a sort of Cinderella, doing practically all the work on the farm. The father rode his horse to market and the pub, nearly always "topping" the market when he took a bullock or pig or some sheep in to sell. His neighbours wondered how he managed to do so well as he never seemed to be at home. They didn't know about the daughter as he didn't tell anybody about her. He told her she would frighten anyone who saw her. Tending the pigs and cleaning out the shippon and digging the potatoes, she looked a bit rough, especially as she had no clothes but the few rags left over from when her mother was alive, over which she wore always a "barass" apron of rough sacking. So if anyone came by, perhaps the hunt, or someone looking for stray sheep, she would hide behind a wall. They sometimes wondered why their horses would shy and stare.

'She used to wish if only she had a fine white apron, like her mother had told her she used to wear for best when she was a girl, then she'd be able to walk to church or put it on when she saw someone riding up the track. Sometimes she got so lonely that she would go up to the little clump of Scots pines above the garden behind the house and climb up one as high as she could till she could see a house over the valley and over the next hill at Sherril — you couldn't see another house from the farmhouse. She would do this even on winter evenings just to see the faint light of a horn lantern at a faraway window.

'One night when her father was away at the pub she did this but this time her feet slipped. She fell, her barass apron caught in a branch, and presumably she was hanged. But when her father next day looked up in the tree beneath which the old yard dog was sitting and whining, he saw just the old barass apron up high in the branches and a great white bird flew from the top of the tree and soared away across the Dart and over the hill.'

Perhaps she had got her white apron at last.

They say you can still see a white bird fly from the pines at Laughter sometimes and if you ride past the old house be ready for your horse to shy...'

PHANTOM COTTAGES

There are many stories of people seeing what are possibly some kind of mirages in Devon, as the one already told of Berry Pomeroy where people saw cottages one day in time past, and on another as they are now. These seem to occur on very hot, still summer days, as Edna White told me when she and her husband had been driving round the lanes between West Ogwell and Bickington. 'Four years ago Harry and I were driving through the back lanes. It was so hot the heat was shimmering from the road, the atmosphere clear as glass. I remember a mother pheasant and her babies in the lane and suddenly we saw this absolutely charming cottage at the side of the road. We slowed down to look at it. It had a little drive up to it and a thatched porch, and stood sideways to the road. It was quite delightful. Later on we went back several times but we never saw it again although we knew exactly where it had stood from various landmarks.'

This spot is near where I live, I walked the lane exactly where she described. There was no sign of any building, but I do know at one time there was a cottage called Heartsease in that area, long since gone.

Another story about a vanishing cottage was told some years ago by two ladies visiting Chagford. During a walk they came across an almost picture book cottage and thought how nice it would be to stay there on their next visit to Devon. They knocked on the door and a little girl answered and showed them into a sitting room. She fetched her mother, who seemed a very cultured and well-dressed lady to live in such a remote and small cottage and to take in guests. However she said she would be delighted to accommodate them if they came back in the autumn, at the moment all her rooms were taken.

A few days later they returned to check the dates. They found all the landmarks in the immediate vicinity, but where the cottage had stood was a pile of rubble overgrown with nettles and brambles, undisturbed for years.

Another fascinating story is told by Stella Robinson of Shaldon who, some years ago had gone to the house of Neil and Wyn Hare to nurse the latter during the birth of her third child. She had not met them before and knew nothing of the family. A few days after the birth she told me the following: 'Wyn said how sorry she was her mother was not there to see the new baby — she had died nine months before — she had been so fond of babies. A few days later as I lay in bed with the baby in its cot beside me, I thought of what she had said and suddenly I saw an elderly lady standing nearby, a smile on her face as she leant forward to peep at the babe. She was dressed in black with grey stockings, a pale and slightly sallow complexion and iron grey hair. She disappeared as suddenly as she had come. On the corner of the pillow in the cot were five bunches of violets. As I bent to pick them up they vanished too. When I told Wyn what had happened, she said "Your description fits my mother in every detail". It seems when the mother died Wyn and her sister Marjorie, and the two children, had put a wreath of violets on their granny's grave — they were her favourite flowers. Stella added, 'I found it a most happy and interesting experience.'

And so is this one, told in the *Transactions* by Theo Brown. The story is taken from the diary of a Mrs Carbonell who died in 1961 leaving a number of papers and photographs to her daughter, Mrs Hartnoll, amongst which was a notebook in which the following incident was recorded.

'In 1932 I was on the committee of the Devon Exploration and Archaeological Society, which in June of that year formed a sub committee to undertake excavations at Frithelstock Priory ruins which adjoin the east end of the parish church. I drove to the priory with my daughter and her small son aged seven. We left the car in the road and walked down the main path to the church and followed it along the south wall to the wicket gate at the east end. The child, Christopher, was running ahead and got to the ruin first. He stood just inside crying, "Oh lovely. I am glad we've come, I love this place!" I said, "You've never been here before and neither has your mother." Christopher looked at me and said emphatically, "I have been here before, long long ago when I was a very old man," and before his mother and I could get over our surprise, he ran to the west end of the ruin and cried out in a most moving tone, "Oh what have they done to my lovely tower with the stairs that went up

74

windey to where I pulled the bell?'' He climbed a grassy heap and looked into the sky, ''and the roof — where's that?''

'His mother said ''You have never been here before, Christopher.'' There was no mistaking the look of puzzlement on his face and bewilderment as he said, ''When I was here long long ago I rang the bell. Oh my lovely tower!''

'We watched him for a moment as he stood, and then, with an entire change of mood and manner, he ran off, and quite naturally began to play about among the fallen masonry in a perfectly normal way any small boy would.

'We examined the prints we had. None showed a tower, and you would hardly expect to find one sandwiched between the south wall of a priory and the east end of the parish church.

'But that is exactly what the excavators did find, and it is shown on the plan on plate 4 of the report in the proceedings of the *Devonshire Association Transactions,* following an item in the notebook dated 1956, vol.108 1976.'

Black dogs are common Dartmoor hauntings. Maybe because at one time Squire Cabell who was lord of the manor of Brooke in Buckfastleigh kept a pack of black hounds for use with the local hunt, and they would answer the sound of the horn on hunting days, returning to their kennels at his house when the day's sport was over. Perhaps one or two of these turned rogue, got lost, wandered off and became vicious. Almost certainly the basis for the story, *The Hound of the Baskervilles,* came from this source, and after Cabell's death it was said his figure still haunted the moor. Mr Honeywill of Ipplepen told me that Conan Doyle stayed at Park Hill House on the Totnes road in sight of his bungalow. He used to walk on the moor with the people he stayed with, and when he tired the coach took them up. The name of the coach driver was Baskerville. He was delighted that Conan Doyle used it in his book. However the villagers were not so delighted for his host took the writer to church with him. He was a Spiritualist, very interested in the Occult, having written a History of Spiritualism, the Holmes stories being merely conceived to augment his income from an unsuccessful medical practice! At one time he got so fed up with Sherlock that he killed him off in 1894, but by popular request he was persuaded to resurrect him for several further volumes!

As I write I hear that several Americans who are descended from Richard Cabell are coming over to visit his grave in the church at

Buckfastleigh where he was buried in 1653 under a twelve foot tomb to keep his evil spirit in its proper place! The tomb has become almost a ruin and the vicar is trying to raise the money to repair it. The memorial was requested by Cabell who said he would continue to terrorise people on the moor until it was completed. Mr Percy Braund of Broadhempston told me his uncle, who at one time lived at Sherril, had to ride for help to Buckfastleigh for a sick animal and on his return through Hembury woods in the dark he heard the huge black dog padding along behind him in the dead leaves.

Another black dog is said to attack people walking from Princetown to Plymouth, so Emily Clay of Brixham told me, flying at their throats. It was discovered a man had been murdered on the spot where this happens, his dog being the only witness, and since when he has been trying to avenge his master.

The hound of Dean Wood is a familiar who lives at the foot of the waterfall. He is said to appear every day at the stroke of noon and midnight. It seems a weaver called Knowles lived in an isolated half-ruined cottage and became hard and bitter as a result, saying why should he have to work so hard while others seemed to make fortunes with far less skill and diligence. When he died his soul could not rest and although spiders spun their webs over the windows, weeds grew up the walls of the cottage, anyone peeping through the window could see the weaver still at work. Anxious locals called on the village priest to set his soul at rest. Prayers were said, but to no avail, he was still seen at work. Eventually the Devil took him to the wood and turned him into a black hound, giving him a nutshell with a hole in it, leading him to the pool and telling him when he had emptied it, then he could rest! Some years ago a whole pack of hounds were led by the fox into Dean Wood. Some of them slipped into the pool and four of them never got out, so perhaps Knowles, the black hound, is at least no longer a lonely shadow!

Then of course there are all the headless horses drawing phantom coaches. At Dunsford in the Teign Valley there were local squires called Fulford going back to the time of Richard I, boasting an un-broken male line, always King's men and forceful characters. In fact one old squire was not satisfied with the way his family had conduct-ed his burial and, according to village lore, has spent the years since trying to get back to the house to tell them! But he is only allowed to proceed a short distance at 12 o'clock on a certain night of the year. He drives in a coach drawn by four headless horses, finding progress difficult as without heads the horses also have no bits and so he holds no reins! To make things worse the harness is on back to front!

Many wild and bloody deeds were perpetrated among the wild and barbarous tinning fraternity of the moor in bygone years. Stone circles may well have been scenes of rough justice, of sacrifice and ritual murder. May be certain emanations are liberated in such places. There are many claims that materialisation can take place from freshly spilled blood. So perhaps I may end this part of my book as in the *Ancient Mariner*. 'Like one that on a lonesome road doth walk in fear and dread and having once turned round walks on and turns no more his head because he knows some fearsome fiend doth close behind him tread. . . '

UFOs

My final chapter in the saga of Devon Mysteries brings us right up to date with the many sightings in the county of Unidentified Flying Objects. My intention is to give both sides of this vexed question: from members of the Aetherius Society, many hundreds of whom have seen these objects, and from a retired science master in Exeter, Mr Western, who kindly gave his time to talk to me from a purely scientific point of view which is entirely his own.

But first I must quote from a book I found in the library entitled *Flying Saucers Over The West* by A.W.Bearne of Southfield Avenue, Paignton. Mr Bearne's son, D.P.Bearne, kindly gave me permission to use parts of this fascinating booklet. He told me his father had died five years ago, adding 'I am interested to hear of your project and you are welcome to quote from my father's book.'

It is dated July 1968 and I should dearly have liked to use all of it, but here is what space will allow. On Monday 30 October 1950 Mr Bearne saw a flying saucer and his first reaction was to make this sighting known generally. He did actually report it to the Paignton police and the editor of the local paper, but at that time gave up the idea of publishing his story in full because it was obvious few people would believe, or take an interest in it. However eventually he did so and included many reports from other sources such as Air Force personnel, and he writes in his foreword, 'I cannot think any intelligent person after reading these reports can fail to realise that flying saucers do exist and are not fictitious.'

To go back to the event itself. It was about 10.30 p.m. as he was walking towards the rear of his home in Southfield Avenue, Paignton, that he saw a light high over his head and a funnel shaped stream of flames, chiefly white, descending, pointed end first, in an absolutely silent and very peculiar manner. The point of the flames seemed to be creeping or 'fingering' downwards. After about half a minute it disappeared from his sight below the top of the roof of the house. Then it came into view again like a ball of fire and instead of travelling downwards as it had been, it now moved horizontally over Paignton towards Churston Ferrers and Higher Brixham at about 500 feet. Then suddenly it took an upward course and ahead of the flames appeared the forward portion of a huge disc from which the flames appeared to recede as it climbed upwards.

Unfortunately by the time he had called his family it had disappeared, but as he said, he had had a scientific upbringing, his father having made and operated for local medical men an X-ray apparatus in the days when there had been none available in the Torbay area. He was also an amateur astronomer so that it was difficult to describe his feelings as he thought how interested his father would have been to witness such an event.

The *Herald Express* of 31 October 1950 carried the following report in the late news column: 'Flying Saucer seen at Paignton. First report of flying saucer seen over the West Country came this afternoon from Mr A.W.Bearne of Southfield Avenue, Paignton.'

The paper then described what he had seen, and on the following day, 1 November, reports started to come in from other eye witnesses, too many alas to give in full, but they did stress that there was no noise, and a trail of fire streamed from the back. Mr F.C. Bray, a fisherman, saw it from the bunk of his boat in Torquay outer harbour. Mr H.Cove Clark of 9, Marine Drive, Paignton, rang Mr Bearne to tell him he had seen a similar occurrence in 1945 when he had been a Special Constable. The crew of a liberty boat from HMS *Defiance* in Devonport Dockyard saw it. On Sunday 5 November the *Sunday Despatch* printed an account of the sighting and said that independent witnesses from places as far apart as Woolacombe, Exeter, Cullompton, Sidmouth and Paignton had seen the saucer. On 13 and 28 December 1950 The *Herald Express* gave two further reports of sightings, first by two cowmen in Kingswear, and then by three men in Penzance. In the *Herald Express* of 2 November 1954 two Torquay men were reported to have seen about fifteen mysterious balls of fire in the sky. One of them, Mr J.Branson of 50, Bampfylde Road, said he had been at Babbacombe the previous day at 3.45 when he saw a cluster of flying objects like balls of fire in the direction of Weymouth. On the following day more and more witnesses came forward to confirm these reports including Mr S.J. Hines of Stover Golf Club, Newton Abbot, who had been on the esplanade at Exmouth when he too had seen similar objects in the Weymouth direction.

At the end of his book Mr Bearne says, 'Many years ago an elderly friend of my father's erected on a quarry cliff property, which he owned, a large board and painted thereon the words, "The End not here or now." He was an intelligent man, a retired naval commander, and it is evident from the foregoing that he was convinced life continues after our earthly existence, in another sphere where a greater knowledge will be ours — and many of us believe as he did.'

By one of those quirks of Fate which indeed make truth stranger than fiction, a day or two after reading Mr Bearne's book I saw in the *Mid Devon Advertiser* of 9 February 1979 the following heading: 'BOOMS: UFO THEORY'. The story read: 'The Concorde booms mystery deepened this week as a UFO expert put forward a startling new theory. It came as British Airways and Ministry of Defence spokesmen denied that Concorde was responsible for every boom or bang heard over South Devon. This was backed up by Mr Robert Wyse, Press Officer at the Torbay UFO Centre, who said that the booms and bangs, often heard late at night, could not be attributable to Concorde . . . it is quite possible they are caused by unidentified flying objects which like Concorde travel at supersonic speed. Records kept by the Centre show that noises have been recorded when it was known that for some reason both Concordes were grounded . . . he added that the Centre has had a number of UFO sightings recorded recently including one seen over Newton Abbot 3 weeks ago. . . '

And so I went to see Mr Wyse who most kindly gave me details of literally dozens of sightings and occurrences connected with UFOs in Devon, some of which I now give.

On 14 April 1978 Mrs June Amos in Tavistock saw a saucer-shaped craft which hovered over the town in a halo of light for three minutes as if observing Dartmoor, and a lady in Plymouth and her two sons saw the same object at the same time. In March the same year Stephen Wright and Paul Groves, members of the UFO Centre in Torquay on sky watch at Watcombe, saw orange lights moving over Teignmouth. On 2 April several members of the Centre saw an object moving from Stoke-in-Teignhead towards Babbacombe and out to sea, describing it as a large circular object with three white lights rotating at the centre. On 10 May Mr and Mrs McClusky were awoken at Haytor, where they live, by a loud rumbling noise at

8 a.m. They saw two orange objects stationary on the hill at the back of their house; one moved off at great speed with the noise of a rocket, then the other followed. Several villagers also heard it and later two jet planes appeared on the scene and followed the course of the UFOs.

In May six members of the UFO Centre were on Haytor at 9.40 p.m. and saw an object flare up, return to its original size and then disappear. And so it went on all through 1978 from Mary Tavy to Bovey Tracey, Dartmouth, Denbury and Woolacombe with reports of sightings, but perhaps the most remarkable story of all is the one told by the two policemen who chased a flying object for fourteen miles.

Two patrolmen, Clifford Waycott and Robert Willey were driving along the A3072 between Okehampton and Holsworthy when they saw this thing in the sky. It was behaving almost as if it had seen them and was waiting for their reaction. It sailed a little way ahead of them above the treetops, so low and silent it could not have been an aircraft. They radioed their HQ and said they were going to investigate. The faster they moved the faster the object moved until they were doing 90 mph. The squad car streaked round corners, climbed hills and swooped down valleys — but they never got nearer than about 400 yards.Eventually they decided to slow down not wishing to report a crashed police car while chasing a UFO! The RAF station at Chivenor denied this occurrence could have had anything to do with them, and they knew of no aircraft which could fit the description given or match the performance of hovering and changing to such supersonic speed. Within 48 hours many more reliable witnesses had also seen objects in the sky of the same type, more police and the BBC engineers manning the transmitter on Dartmoor among them.

But perhaps an even more odd and macabre mystery is the one written up by Ursula Wright. Fifteen ponies were found dead on a Dartmoor beauty spot by Mr Hicks of the Livestock Protection Society on 11 April while walking the Cherrybrook Valley. Four of these were grouped together and eventually the other eleven were found only a matter of days later. There was nothing to explain how they died or why they were in such a close group. Police and RSPCA investigated within 48 hours but already the bodies were largely decomposed. Why had carcases almost whole on 11 April been reduced to little more than skeletons in 48 hours, a mystery in itself said Tony Booth, Chief Inspector of the RSPCA.

One theory put forward was that they died of redworm, but that would not result in broken necks and legs. Another that they were poisoned by eating bog asphodel, small yellow flowers found on Dartmoor. Then five UFO investigators including Mr and Mrs Wyse were called in. Accompanied by the press and BBC TV, and using metal detectors, they hoped to find some evidence that the deaths might be due to visits from extraterrestrial beings. Mr Wyse told me, 'After four hours we found no clues whatever. It was a useful experience in fieldwork, and did rule out the possible explanation that the ponies had been shot as there was no trace of any metal. On a second visit in August we took teeth from the skeletons; these came away from the jawbones with more than usual ease and a hoof disintegrated when picked up.' Eventually Mr Wyse put his conclusions before members of the South Devon Technical College: the only verdict they could reach was that it seemed the ponies had been crushed by something from the air.

Then there was the Chapman Incident. Frank Chapman, ex RAF pilot was at home on the evening of 12 December 1977 with a friend John Hanley. Oddly enough they had been discussing UFOs when suddenly they saw a blue pulsating light in the sky coming from the direction of Oreston, SSE to NNW. It stopped, hovered, then reversed along its path towards Torquay. It picked up speed to about 250 mph and then shot upwards at an angle of 55 degrees with no sound. Frank Chapman estimated the object was at a height of about 5,000 feet and three times the size of a Lightning fighter. He also estimated that during its final acceleration it must have gone through 10g force. He was certain it was intelligently controlled.

Once more in September 1978 there was a spate of sightings in the Exeter area reported in the *Exeter Weekly News* of Friday 22 September. The reports sent many people running to the hills to search the skies for airborne lights, every night swarms of people gathering on the heights around the city, but Tiverton topped the list for close encounters. Police had to be called to Seven Crosses near the town to deal with traffic jams; sometimes fifty or more people spent the night on the hill where they caused congestion in the narrow country lanes.

It seems a lorry driver by the name of David Coleman started the excitement in Tiverton when he saw a light hanging on the horizon over Seven Crosses for several nights, twenty feet above a clump of trees. 'Suddenly three lights came on', he said, 'and appeared to be shining right at me. I was petrified but could not take my eyes off them as they moved down the valley out of sight.'

Confirmation of the sightings at Tiverton came from three women at Bradninch and the British Flying Saucer Bureau also reported an increase in UFO sightings throughout the South West. At the same time rumours in the Exeter area said that fields and hedges had been found scorched following the landings of mysterious machines from outer space, but enquiries made by the *Exeter Weekly News* brought no actual eye witnesses to confirm such reports.

I also called to see Mrs Joy Greatrex who is the representative of the Aetherius Society in Torquay. She let me listen to a tape of a lecture given by the Reverend Ray Nielsen, the world's leading authority on Flying Saucer Contact, who is in constant touch with the latest developments on this front, presenting their information to the public through nationwide campaigns. The lecture is fascinating, but I can here only mention that Ray Nielsen spoke much of Doctor George King who is a prominent scientist and Western Master of Yoga. For over twenty years he has been the Primary Earth Channel for teachings from People from other Planets.

In his book, *You Are Responsible*, on flying saucers, he gives twenty messages which have been transmitted to earth by Cosmic Intelligence, revealing fact after fact concerning the highly advanced civilisations existing on other planets in this Solar System. Many prophecies of advanced scientific discovery and of flying saucers made by space intelligence themselves in the 1950s are given, every one of which was later verified in the media throughout the world.

Their theory is that these spacecraft which visit the earth are physical vehicles manned by extraterrestrial intelligences of a very much more advanced evolutionary status than we are. They tap the natural source of power which exists throughout the whole solar system and they have chosen George King as a communication channel because of his knowledge and ability in the deeper aspects of Yoga. These space people are intelligences who have gone through our stage of evolution and the Society assert that visitors from other worlds have set foot on this planet in human form. They have come to help man through this particular phase of evolution, for in their opinion we are slowly poisoning ourselves beyond the point of no return. Also they are here to learn from us about our environment so they may help us, by being among us, by using our bodies and looking like earth people.

Whether you choose to believe all I have written above or not is up to you, but I think I must end this very brief look at their beliefs with a story told by George King. Two ladies were placed in a Government Department in America, ladies from outer space that is, as filing clerks. They were of course excellent at their jobs and elevated into the Missing Persons Bureau of the FBI. With their full psychic abilities they proceeded to find everyone who was missing and the work of the Bureau dwindled rapidly. They were of course regarded with suspicion and had to leave in a great hurry!

If you find this a bit much for your credence, let me bring you back to earth, literally, by introducing you to Mr W.G.Western of Exeter to get his views on this subject. He said, 'It was really the sightings in New Zealand which started my interest. I was talking to this fellow from Huntingdon who said he had seen things similar to these mentioned near the power station at Great Barford, small balls of light dancing around. I was intrigued as I once lived in that area — and I began to think about UFOs. I'd never really thought about them before. I began to think there must be some rational explanation and then suddenly I thought — ionisation. Could this be due to some form of bombardment by cosmic rays, or any kind of electrical force?'

I am not going to repeat all that Mr Western said to me as it is far too technical, although of absorbing interest, but in plain English as I see it, his idea is that the analysis of UFO sightings can be seen mostly as explicable misinterpretations such as Venus, aircraft lights, or similar causes, but inevitably there are a few left over which cannot be easily explained. Glowing shapes of differing sizes, spherical or cylindrical, which can be stationary and yet given to incredible acceleration and also radar reflecting. He said: 'I have waited for physicists to offer a possible answer in terms of what we know about the atmosphere and ionosphere, but have not heard any suggestions, so with all humility I offer an hypothesis. Ionised layers exist around the earth at altitudes from 100 to 400 kilometres. Normally the ionisation is insufficient to reflect radio waves at VHF but on occasions patches of high ionisation occur at the lower limit which will reflect even VHF waves. These patches vary from something which is very small such as 100 metres across to areas of many kilometres. They are known to radio enthusiasts as Sporadic E

84

because the former Heaviside Layer is now known as the E layer. They vary in speed of travel and can move at high speed with sudden acceleration. At ground level we get the occurrence of St Elmo's Fire when the level of electric charge locally around a pointed object becomes so high that the air around it glows . . . Could not local patches of atmosphere also become so heavily charged and ionised that they not only reflect radar waves but also glow and drift sporadically like patches of Sporadic E? Thunder balls which often occur in old folklore and legend (see my story of Widecombe and Rowbrook) going through houses — ionised air . . . If you get thunderbolts or thunder balls, highly electrified objects with a strong electric charge, and then they find a pointed object, however small, electric charges congregate round it and draw a stream of electrons from it, preferring pointed things to round. This is why you are warned not to go out on a level plain with an umbrella, or shelter under a tree in a thunderstorm. Iron and metal in the soil will attract — the positive charges tend to congregate round anything that is sticking up . . .'

So we have come full circle from the days of long, long ago on Dartmoor when thunderballs struck. Now it is flying saucers — UFOs — that we see over the countryside, all part of our unsolved Devon mysteries.

ALSO AVAILABLE

OCCULT IN THE WEST
by Michael Williams

Michael Williams follows his successful **Supernatural in Cornwall** with further interviews and investigations into the Occult — this time incorporating Devon. Ghosts and clairvoyancy, dreams and psychic painting, healing and hypnosis are only some of the facets of a fascinating story that will make even the Doubting Thomases think hard. 'The Devil's footprints claim in Devon', he says, 'is a mystery in the Agatha Christie class . . . and it's fact, not fiction!'

AUTUMN 1979
ISBN 0 906456 15 0   Price £1.50.

ALSO BY JUDY CHARD

ALONG THE DART
34 photographs and 2 maps. Price 75p.
Judy Chard takes us on a journey up the River Dart from historic Dartmouth and the sea to its beginning on Dartmoor. It is a journey lovingly and vividly told.
"*. . . full of facts, anecdotes, and legends about the river and its surrounding area and people . . .*"   Roy Derwent, Express & Echo

ALONG THE LEMON
35 photographs. Price 95p.
Judy Chard puts one of Devon's lesser-known rivers on the map.
"*. . . in prose and pictures, the story of the river from its rising near Haytor, its junction with the Sig and final pouring into the Teign.*"
     Herald Express

"*. . . a book with exceptional sparkle . . .*"

     Devon Life

ABOUT WIDECOMBE

by Judy Chard. 43 photographs. Price 90p.

This is a personal portrait of the beautiful Devonshire village. There are interviews with characters like Uncle Tom Cobley and the Widecombe Wag, researches into Widecombe's colourful past, including its world-famous Fair and Song.

'. . . ranges over the history of Widecombe with an absorbing look at its characters, past and present . . .'
Mid-Devon Advertiser

'A warmly recommended read for all who love Devon — and Dartmoor in particular.'
The Independent

OTHER BOSSINEY TITLES INCLUDE

DARTMOOR PRISON

by Rufus Endle. 35 photographs. Price 90p.

A vivid portrait of the famous prison on the moor stretching from 1808 — with rare photographs taken inside today.

'. . . enjoyable and entertaining throughout . . .'
James Mildren, Western Morning News

'. . . a rare photographic peep into the interior . . . and a fascinating insight into its life and history . . .'
Jean Kenzie, Tavistock Gazette

'the bleak Devon cage's 170 year history . . . fascinatingly sketched by one of the Westcountry's best known journalists Rufus Endle . . . the man with the key to Dartmoor.'
Western Daily Press

MY DARTMOOR

by Clive Gunnell of Westward TV — television's most famous walker. Price £1.50.

Map and 12 pages of photographs and drawings of Dartmoor wildlife by Robin Armstrong. Introduction by Jeremy Thorpe.

'The work is that of a merry man, and an observant, though kindly one.'
Western Morning News

THE BARBICAN

by Elizabeth Gunnell, 32 photographs. Price 75p.

'Anyone with a love for old Plymouth and the waterfront should not miss this lovely little book. It is outstanding value and highly recommended.'
Tavistock Gazette

TOTNES

by Elizabeth Gunnell, 32 illustrations. Price 75p.

Elizabeth Gunnell follows the success of her Barbican story with an immensely readable guide about Totnes, one of the oldest boroughs in Britain.

"We meet historic people cheek-by-jowl with moderns . . . they all step out of the pages equally alive."
Devon Life

TO TAVISTOCK GOOSIE FAIR
by Clive Gunnell. 41 photographs. Price 75p.
A look at one of the historic Fairs in the Westcountry from the inside — the author himself lives at Tavistock.

ABOUT EXMOOR AND NORTH DEVON
by Ronald Duncan, 15 photographs and map. Price 75p.
"You will find this book well-informed, well-written, well-illustrated and provocative."   The John Blunt Column
". . . suggested routes across some of the loveliest stretches of the Westcountry."
                                                                                              Western Daily Press

KING ARTHUR COUNTRY in CORNWALL, THE SEARCH for the REAL ARTHUR
by Brenda Duxbury, Michael Williams and Colin Wilson.
Over 50 photographs and 3 maps. Paperback £1.20, hardcovers £2.95.
An exciting exploration of the Arthurian sites in Cornwall and Scilly, including the related legends of Tristan and Iseult, with The Search for the Real Arthur by Colin Wilson.
'. . . the best Bossiney book so far.'   Cornish Life
'Filled with the most beautiful photographs . . . brings to life the romantic legend . . .'   Desmond Lyons, Cornwall Courier

MY CORNWALL
A personal vision of Cornwall by eleven writers living and working in the county: Daphne du Maurier, Ronald Duncan, James Turner, Angela du Maurier, Jack Clemo, Denys Val Baker, Colin Wilson, C.C. Vyvyan, Arthur Caddick, Michael Williams and Derek Tangye with reproductions of paintings by Margo Maeckelberghe and photographs by Bryan Russell.   Price £1.50.
"An ambitious collection of chapters."   The Times, London

CORNWALL & SCILLY PECULIAR
by David Mudd, 48 photographs. Price £1.00.
David Mudd uses his perceptive eye and his pride of all things Cornish to write entertainingly, at times with humour, but always affectionately, of some of the people, events, values and beliefs that create the background to Cornwall's strange and compelling charm.
". . . one of the most important Cornish titles produced by Bossiney . . ."
                                                                                              The Cornishman

BOTH SIDES OF TAMAR
Devon & Cornwall portrayed in words and pictures. 24 illustrations. Price 50p.
Chapters by John Betjeman, Charles Causley, J.C. Trewin, Clive Gunnell, Tom Salmon, E.W. Martin, Bill Best Harris, James Turner, Jane Toplis and Arthur Caddick.
". . . a memorable book on Devon and Cornwall."   Western Morning News